Eyewitness
MEDIEVAL
LIFE

Merchant's coin box

Writing quills

Horn inkwells

Papal ring

Carved wooden angel from a medieval church nave

Church censer for burning incense

Medieval stone carving of a woman's head

Shepherd's horn pipe

12th-century reliquary casket

Bagpipes

Emblem of the
Virgin Mary

Eyewitness
MEDIEVAL
LIFE

Medieval badge
of Christ

Written by
ANDREW LANGLEY

Photographed by
GEOFF BRIGHTLING & GEOFF DANN

Trestle table

DK Publishing

Harp

Medieval reed
instrument,
or shawm

Spoons
cut from
horn

Decorated
ceramic pitchers
for wine or ale

Wooden
food
bowl

LONDON, NEW YORK, MELBOURNE, MUNICH, and DELHI

Project editor Bridget Hopkinson
Art editor Vicky Wharton
Designer Kati Poynor
Managing editor Gillian Denton
Managing art editor Julia Harris
Researcher Céline Carez
Production Charlotte Trail
Picture research Kathy Lockley
Consultants Peter Brears & Charles Kightly

THIS EDITION
Editors Lorrie Mack, Steve Setford, Jessamy Wood
Art editors Rebecca Johns, Peter Radcliffe
Managing editors Julie Ferris, Jane Yorke
Managing art editors Owen Peyton Jones, Jane Thomas
Associate publisher Andrew Macintyre
Production Andy Hilliard, Jenny Jacoby, Hitesh Patel
Picture research Harriet Mills, Sarah Pownall
DTP designer Siu Yin Ho
Jacket editor Adam Powley
US editor Margaret Parrish

This Eyewitness ® Guide has been conceived by
Dorling Kindersley Limited and Editions Gallimard

First published in the United States in 1996.
This revised edition published in the United States in 2011
by DK Publishing
375 Hudson Street, New York, New York 10014
Copyright © 1996, 2002, 2011 Dorling Kindersley Limited

11 12 13 14 15   10 9 8 7 6 5 4 3 2 1

175430—05/11

A catalog record for this book is available from the Library of Congress.

ISBN 978-0-7566-7316-1 (Hardcover)
ISBN 978-0-7566-8282-8 (Library Binding)

Color reproduction by Colourscan,
Singapore; MDP, UK

Printed and bound by Toppan Printing Co.
(Shenzhen) Ltd., China

Discover more at
www.dk.com

Stone carving of a man
making a face

"Back" stool

Drinking
vessel

Table settir

Contents

Tester bed

The Middle Ages

THE TERM "MEDIEVAL" COMES from the Latin *medium aevum*, which means "the middle ages." But when were the Middle Ages? Before them came the Classical Age of ancient Greece and Rome, and after came the Renaissance (p. 62). The Middle Ages covered the period roughly in between, from the 5th century to the end of the 15th. In many ways, medieval times seem remote and mysterious, peopled by knights and ladies, kings and bishops, monks and pilgrims. Yet European cities, states, parliaments, banking systems, and universities all have their roots there, and parts of the landscape are still dominated by the great medieval castles and cathedrals.

A LIGHT IN THE DARK
During the Dark Ages, art and learning survived in remote monasteries. This illuminated letter comes from the Book of Kells (c. 800), which was kept at St. Columba's monastery in Ireland.

THE BYZANTINE EMPIRE
When the Roman Empire split in two, the western half, based in Rome, declined, but the eastern half, based in the Byzantine capital of Constantinople (now Istanbul), flourished. Its greatest ruler was the Christian emperor Justinian I (c. 482–565).

Viking brooches

SEA RAIDERS
The Vikings began to raid the coasts of Europe toward the end of the 8th century.

KING OF EUROPE
Charles the Great, or Charlemagne (742–814), united an empire covering much of modern France and Germany. He was a great Christian leader as well as a skillful warrior.

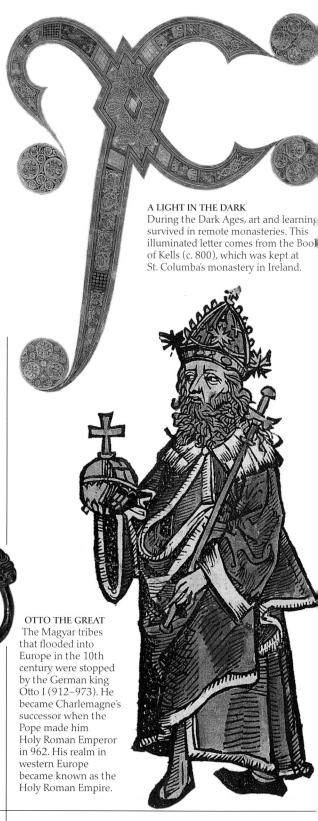

OTTO THE GREAT
The Magyar tribes that flooded into Europe in the 10th century were stopped by the German king Otto I (912–973). He became Charlemagne's successor when the Pope made him Holy Roman Emperor in 962. His realm in western Europe became known as the Holy Roman Empire.

THE DARK AGES
In the 5th century, the Roman Empire slowly fell apart as Germanic tribes from the north pushed across its frontiers, destroying towns and trade routes. Saxons settled in Britain, Franks took over Gaul (France), and Goths invaded Italy itself. In 476, the last Roman emperor lost his throne. The following centuries of disorder became known as the "Dark Ages," but this was not an entirely accurate description. Under the 6th-century emperor Justinian I, the Byzantine capital of Constantinople became one of the most magnificent cities in the world. By the 8th century, the great Frankish ruler Charlemagne had once more united a large part of Europe, encouraging the spread of learning and Christianity throughout his empire.

THE GREAT LEADERS
The Christian king Charlemagne supported the Pope as he tried to drive the barbarian invaders out of Italy, and in 800 the Pope crowned him "Holy Roman Emperor" in gratitude. Europe was threatened by invaders throughout the 9th and 10th centuries— Vikings raided the northern coasts, and the fierce Magyars pressed in from central Asia. But gradually, new nations began to emerge. The lands of the Franks became France, Alfred the Great (c. 846–899) defeated the Vikings to become king of England, and Otto I of Germany fought off the Magyars.

400–800

800–1000

ORMANS NORTH AND SOUTH
s William of Normandy (c. 1027–1087)
was conquering England in 1066, other
Norman nobles were carving out
n empire in Italy and Sicily.

HE CRUSADES
he Crusades (p. 28)
egan in 1095 as a
Christian campaign
o drive the Muslims
ut of Palestine.
erusalem was
aptured in
099, but later
rusades were
unsuccessful.

German
crusader's
helmet

UNIFIER
This beautiful
gilded head
represents the
powerful Holy
Roman emperor
Frederick I,
or Barbarossa
(c. 1121–1190),
who brought
unity to the
German states in
the 12th century.

THE GREAT PLAGUE
The Black Death had a
lasting effect on European
society. So many peasants
died that there were
hardly enough people
left to farm the land.
Increased demands
on their labor
caused the peasants
to revolt in both
France and England.

Bishop's crook,
or crozier

THE CHURCH
The Catholic Church
was one of the most
powerful institutions
of the Middle Ages.
During the 13th
century, the religious
Inquisition was
established to hunt out
those who disagreed
with its teachings.
Those found guilty
could be punished
with excommunication
(being cut off from the
Church) or even death.

RENAISSANCE GENIUS
Michelangelo (1475–1564)
was one of the greatest
Renaissance sculptors.
His most famous work is
the beautiful marble statue,
the *David*, now in Florence.

DISSOLVING THE MONASTERIES
When the English king Henry VIII
(1491–1547) quarreled with the Catholic
Church, he appointed himself head of the
Church in England and "dissolved" the great
monasteries, taking their lands and property.

STABILITY
After 1000, life in Europe became more stable.
Supported by the feudal system (p. 8), strong
rulers brought order to the new nations. This
encouraged trade and the growth of towns and
cities, and the population rose. The Catholic
Church (p. 30) reached the peak of its power as
great cathedrals were built and new monastic
orders were formed (p. 36). The first European
university was founded in Italy.

PLAGUE AND WAR
The 14th century saw a series of disasters
strike Europe. Bad harvests caused famine,
and the Black Death (p. 60) killed one-third
of the population. England and France began
the Hundred Years' War in 1337, and church
leaders squabbled over the title of pope.
However, there was also an expansion in
trade spearheaded in northern Europe by
the prosperous Hanseatic League (p. 47).

NEW BEGINNINGS
The 15th century was a time of change.
Scholars and artists explored new ideas and
artistic styles in the Renaissance (p. 62), and
in the 1500s religious reformers broke away
from the Catholic Church in the Reformation
(p. 62). This was also a great age of discovery.
Explorers from Spain and Portugal crossed
the Atlantic and Indian oceans, opening new
horizons for trade and development (p. 63).

1000–1250

1250–1400

1400–1540

Medieval society

SOCIETY IN MUCH OF MEDIEVAL Europe was organized into a "feudal" system, which was based on the allocation of land in return for services. The king gave grants of land, or fiefs, to his most important noblemen (barons and bishops) and in return, each noble promised to supply the king with soldiers in time of war. A noble pledged himself to be the king's servant, or vassal, at a special ceremony—kneeling before the king he swore an oath of loyalty with the words, "Sire, I become your man." The great nobles often divided their lands among lower lords, or knights, who in turn became their vassals. In this way, feudalism stretched from the top to the bottom of society. At the very bottom were the peasants who worked the land itself. They had few rights, little property, and no vassals.

GOD'S DEPUTY
Medieval kings were seen as God's deputies on Earth. A coronation was a magnificent religious ceremony at which archbishops anointed the new king with holy oil as a sign of his status.

TOP OF THE TREE
In this 14th-century picture, a French king presides over a gathering of his most important vassals, with the bishops on one side and barons on the other.

TAXES NOT AXES
By about 1100, many vassals were unwilling to fight for their king. Instead, they were allowed to pay a sum of cash called "scutage," or shield money, that could be used to hire soldiers. Scutage was one of the first regular money taxes levied by kings from their noblemen. A system of tax-collectors (above) made sure that the full amounts were paid.

THE BARONS
Barons (p.24) were the most powerful and wealthy noblemen, who received their fiefs directly from the king. When William of Normandy (p. 7) conquered England in 1066, he had about 120 barons. Each provided the king with a possible army of more than 5,000 men.

THE PEASANTS
The peasants were at the bottom of the feudal tree. They were the workers who farmed the land to provide food for everyone else. Most peasants worked for a lord who let them farm a piece of land for themselves in return for their labor (p. 10).

THE LORDS
Lords ruled over fiefs or manors (p. 14), renting out most of their land to the peasants who worked for them. They were also the warriors of medieval society. As trained knights, they were bound by oath to serve the great nobles who granted them their fiefs, and they could be called to battle at any time.

Bishop wears a miter as a sign of his status

King is mockingly portrayed with a cat on his head!

THE BISHOPS

Bishops could wield as much power as the barons. They ruled over areas called dioceses (p. 31), and all the priests and monasteries within them. The regular collection of tithes (p. 13) and other taxes from their dioceses made many bishops extremely rich.

THE KING

Few kings had enough wealth to maintain a standing army, so they depended on their barons to provide knights and soldiers. But kings had to work hard to keep their barons under control (p. 26). In many cases, especially in France and Germany, the great barons grew very powerful, and governed their fiefs as independent states.

ROUGH JUSTICE

In the Middle Ages, ordinary people had few rights. Those who broke the law were tried in the court of their lord, who had almost complete power over them. Punishment for crimes was often harsh— a convicted criminal might be dragged behind a horse, whipped, locked in the stocks, or hanged, depending on the nature of his or her crime. But being at the top of the feudal system did not always ensure better treatment. Lords and barons sometimes had to pay their king large sums of money to get a fair trial. The medieval Church operated its own justice system with its own laws (the canon laws) and courts (p. 31) that were outside the jurisdiction of the king.

A peasant's life

Statue of a
French peasant
c. 1500

ACCORDING TO THE LAW, most medieval peasants owned nothing except their own stomachs. Everything—including their land, their animals, their homes, their clothes, and even their food—belonged to the lord of the manor (p. 14). Known as serfs or villeins, peasants were bound to work for their lord, who allowed them to farm their own piece of land in return. Their lives consisted of almost constant toil. Most struggled to produce enough food to feed their families and to fulfill their duties to the lord. Forbidden from leaving the manor without permission, the only way for a peasant to gain freedom was by saving enough money to buy a plot of land, or by marrying a free person.

Simple spoons can be cut from horn

Shepherd's horn pipe

DAILY GRIND
Peasants worked hard every day except Sundays and holy days, in blazing sun, rain, or snow. Combined with a poor diet, it wasn't surprising that many European peasants in 1300 lived no longer than 25 years.

Tired peasant wipes the sweat from his brow

DO IT YOURSEL
Peasants made some of their own too and utensils, although skilled craftsme produced their pottery, leatherwor and iron. Besides wood and leather, th most important material was horn fro cattle or sheep. Light and strong, it di not absorb flavors like wood and did n require great energy to shape (p. 16). Hor spoons saved on dishwashing; according one writer, "with a little licking they w always be kept as clean as a di

Wat Tyler is killed by a blow from a sword

THE PEASANTS' REVOLT
After the Black Death (pp. 60–61), there was a shortage of labor in 14th-century Europe. The peasants had to work harder than ever, and in England they also had to pay an extra tax. In 1381, the English peasants rose in rebellion. Led by Wat Tyler, they marched on London where they murdered the archbishop. When they met the king, Richard II (1367–1400), he agreed to end the new tax, but Wat Tyler was killed in a quarrel. The peasant mob swiftly disbanded and went home. The French Jacquerie revolt of 1358 ended much more bloodily, when armored knights slaughtered several thousand rebels.

Straw hat to protect the head on hot days

Cheap pewter pin for good luck

Felt hat decorated with a rooster feather and a "fleur-de-lys" pin

Brown woolen jacket lined with linen

Blue woolen doublet fastened with laces, or points

Linen shirt

Linen underpants, or braes

Leather flask, or costrel, for carrying ale into the fields

Hose are tied to doublet with points

Peasants working with their hose rolled down

Woolen "split" hose can be rolled down for working

PEASANT COTTAGE
Most peasants lived in simple homes like this reconstructed 13th-century cottage. The walls were made from local flint, but they were more often made from wattle and daub—woven strips of wood covered with a mixture of dung, straw, and clay. Inside, the floor was of bare, trampled dirt. Most cottages had only one or two rooms, which contained basic furniture such as a trestle table and bench, a chest for clothes, and straw mattresses to sleep on. There was a stone hearth in the center of the main room, but no chimney, so it must have been very dark and smoky.

Leather working boot

PLAIN CLOTHES
These are the kind of clothes that would have been worn by a peasant in the 1400s. Clothes, like tools, were mostly homemade from local materials. Peasant women spent much of their time spinning wool into coarse thread, which was then woven into cloth and made into garments. Sheepskin cloaks were worn in winter to keep out the cold and rain, and wooden pattens (p. 23) could be put on over leather boots in muddy conditions. Although outer clothes were never washed, linen underwear was laundered regularly. People's clothes generally smelled of woodsmoke, which had a deodorizing effect!

Tied to the soil

IN MEDIEVAL EUROPE, more than 90 percent of the population lived and worked on the land. Farming was a full-time job, since methods were ancient and not very efficient. The crop-growing areas around a village were usually divided into three big fields. Peasants were allotted some land in each so that good and bad soil was divided equally. They hoed and harvested their own plots, or strips, but worked together on big jobs such as plowing and hay-making. A failed harvest could mean starvation for the whole village.

Wooden pitchfork for lifting hay and sheaves of wheat

HARVEST TIME
In late summer, women and children worked alongside the men to bring in the harvest. They cut the wheat with sickles, grasping each clump firmly so that the grains wouldn't shake loose. The wheat was then tied in bundles, or sheaves, set in stooks in the field to ripen, loaded onto a cart, and taken to the barn. Once the harvest was in, the wheat was threshed—beaten with a hinged stick, or flail, to loosen the grains from the ears.

SOWING THE SEED
In the "three-field system," only two fields were sown with crops in one year while the third was left empty, or fallow, so it could recover its fertility. One field was sown with wheat in winter; the next spring, the second was sown with rye, barley, or oats. Seeds were scattered, or broadcast, by hand.

Man knocking acorns out of an oak tree for his pigs

Seeds fall in the plowed furrows, but many are lost to hungry birds

Farmer broadcasts the seeds in a sweeping arc

Basket of seeds called a seedlip

Shafts for pulling the cart

FALL ACORNS
Every fall, the lord of the manor allowed his serfs to run their pigs in his private woods, where they could feed on acorns and beechnuts. Sheep, geese, and goats grazed on common wasteland at the edge of the village. All the same, most animals were thin and wiry!

Hungry pig

Peasants working together at harvest time

SHEAR PROFIT
Sheep shearing was the most important spring job in hilly regions of medieval Europe. Wool fetched high prices, and the wool trade became one of the richest industries of the Middle Ages.

TITHE BARN
This huge 13th-century barn was used to store tithes. Villagers had to give the local priest a tenth, or tithe, of everything they produced, from crops and firewood, to eggs and flour. Tithes made some churches very wealthy—and very unpopular.

MANUAL LABOR
With no machines, all farm work was done by hand using simple tools like these. Most jobs involved backbreaking labor, from breaking clods (lumps of soil) to hoeing young crops.

Billhook for maintaining hedges

Sickle for harvesting crops

Threshed wheat stalks, or straw

Rear gate is tied to keep the straw from falling out

Rim of wooden wheel is clad with six iron "strakes" for extra strength

CARTED OFF
Medieval peasants would have transported their wheat, straw, and hay in carts like this. Straw (the leftover stalks from the harvest) was used for numerous purposes, from thatching roofs to making mattresses. Hay was another important crop. Along with wheatstraw and dried beans, it provided the only winter feed for farm animals. Even then, there was rarely enough to go around and most cattle, pigs, and goats had to be killed in late fall. Every peasant had a share in the village's hay meadow, and hay-making was a communal task.

Large wheels allow the cart to ride over big bumps and ruts

Running a manor

M OST COUNTRY PEOPLE LIVED on a manor that consisted of a village, the lord's house or castle, a church, and the surrounding farmland. The lord of the manor governed the community and appointed officials who made sure that the villagers performed their duties. These involved farming the lord's land, or demesne, and paying rents in the form of produce. The lord also acted as a judge in the manor court, and had the power to fine those who broke the law. Since manors were often isolated, the villagers had to produce everything they needed themselves. Few goods, except salt for curing meat, and iron for tools, came from outside. The only visitors were pedlars, pilgrims, or soldiers, and few people ever traveled far from their own village.

OTHER DUTIES
The lord was, first and foremost, a knight (p. 8) who provided men to fight for the king whenever he needed them. These knights are receiving their swords.

Steward discusses farm business with his lord

Medieval watering pot

THE STEWARD
The lord left the daily running of his manor to a number of officials. The most important was the steward, who organized farmwork, kept accounts of the estate's money, and presided at the manor court if his master was away. Stewards were well-paid, powerful figures in the district.

THE LORD AND LADY
The lord and lady of the manor had to oversee the running of the estate and their household, but they also had a fair amount of free time to pursue leisure activities. This French tapestry shows two angels holding a canopy over the heads of a noble and his lady, perhaps symbolizing their charmed lives.

THE MANOR HOUSE
The lord and his family lived in a large house that was often built of stone. It was surrounded by gardens and stables, and was protected by a high wall and sometimes by a moat. Aside from the church, the manor house was the center of community life—its great hall served as the manor court, and as the venue for special village feasts, such as those given after the harvest and at Christmastime.

Favorite hawks were carried everywhere, even into church!

HAPPY HUNTING
Lords and ladies spent much of their time hunting, which was considered a noble pursuit. Many kept hawks to fly after rabbits and doves, and packs of hounds for chasing deer or wild boar in their private woodland.

GOING TO THE MILL
In most communities, there was only one watermill, which was owned by the lord. He banned all others, even handmills, so that the villagers were forced to carry their grain to his mill for grinding into flour. As payment, the lord kept some of their grain. Villagers might also have to bake their bread in the lord's oven and use his wine press for their grapes, for which they paid similar fees.

THE BAILIFF
Next in importance to the steward was the bailiff. He was usually a peasant, which can be seen from his clothes (right)—they were made from better cloth than those of a farm laborer, but were basically the same style. However, the bailiff was not a serf (p. 10), but a freeholder who owned his own land. He was in charge of allotting jobs to the peasants, looking after the demesne's cattle, and taking care of repairs to buildings and tools, for which he hired skilled craftsmen such as carpenters and smiths.

THE REEVE
The reeve was the bailiff's right-hand man. He was a peasant, chosen by the other villagers. Carrying a white stick as a badge of office, the reeve supervised work on the lord's demesne, checking that everyone began on time, and ensuring that none of the produce was stolen.

Peak keeps sunlight out of the eyes and, when reversed, allows rainwater to run off

Felt hat

Brown doublet

Woolen, linen-lined jacket with pewter buttons

Jacket has a longer cut than that of a laborer's jacket

Stirrups pulled the hose closer to the leg for a fashionably slender silhouette

Leather boots

A medieval home

KEEPING WARM
Medieval homes had hearths in the center of the room—away from wooden walls to minimize the risk of fire. By the 1400s, more people could afford stone chimneys, so fireplaces were more common.

MEDIEVAL HOMES WERE VERY DIFFERENT FROM OURS. Peasants spent most of the daylight hours outside, so the drafts and little light from the unglazed windows did not trouble them. Inside, they kept below the smoke of the fire by sitting on low stools. For lighting, they peeled field rushes and dipped them in fat, which made them burn like small candles. Everything was kept as clean as possible—the dirt floors were often worn hollow as a result of constant sweeping. Domestic life was much more communal than ours, with whole families eating, sleeping, and spending free time together in their one- or two-roomed houses (p. 11). The homes of the wealthy were much more elaborate. By the 13th century, some noblemen had a private family room, the solar. They paved their floors with decorated tiles and hung bright tapestries on their walls.

Shutters are closed at night

Unwound horn

Central part is split and polished

WINDOW ON THE WORLD
It was possible to judge the social status of a household by looking at its windows. The poor had small holes covered with wooden shutters that could be closed at night or in cold weather. The better-off might have fenestral windows—lattice frames covered in linen that had been soaked in resin and tallow. These let in light and kept out drafts, and could be removed on sunny days.

Curly sheep's horn

HORN OF PLENTY
Horn has been called the plastic of the Middle Ages because it was cheap and pliable. To make a horn window pane, the horn was first softened in water for three months, then unwound, split, and polished until it was transparent.

Urinal; urine was often saved to be used for cloth finishing and dyeing processes

Wattle-and-daub wall (p. 11)

Some castle privies emptied directly into the moat!

THE SMALLEST ROOM
By the late 15th century, many houses had an indoor privy. It was little more than a closet in the wall with a hole over a cesspit. There probably would have been an outdoor privy as well.

Horn panes are slotted into a wooden window frame

GLASS SUBSTITUTE
In the Middle Ages, glass was rare and expensive and only churches or royal palaces could afford glass windows. Noblemen and merchants often made do with windows made from panes of polished horn. These were cheaper and tougher than glass and let in lots of light, although they were a bit difficult to see through.

ROCK-A-BYE BABY
This noble baby's rocking cradle was probably the most comfortable bed in the house. However, infancy was a dangerous time—more than one in three babies died, usually from disease.

Cradle can be rocked by mother's foot while she sews or spins

SEATS TO SUIT
In most homes, people sat on plain stools or benches. Only a lord was likely to have a chair with a back and armrests, and he was thus called the "chairman."

Canopy is attached to the ceiling

BEDTIME
A 15th-century servants' book gives strict instructions on putting the lord to bed. After undressing him, combing his hair and pulling on his nightcap, the servant should, "draw the curtains round about the bed, set there his night-light, drive out the dog and cat, giving them a clout, take no leave of your lord, but bow low to him and retire."

White rose of the Virgin Mary; many decorations bore religious motifs

Canopy, or tester

HANGINGS
Painted linen, woven tapestries, and fine wool cloths were hung from walls and doorways. They made rooms warmer by keeping out drafts and providing insulation. They also added brightness to dim interiors. This doorway and painted linen wall-hanging come from the home of a wealthy merchant.

Warm, woolen curtains keep out drafts

Linen pillow stuffed with chopped straw

Linen sheet

Woven straw mattress

Lavender *Tansy* *Ladies' bedstraw*

KEEPING BUGS AT BAY
Herbs such as lavender, tansy, and ladies' bedstraw were strewn on straw mattresses. Their strong scents not only made the bed smell sweeter, but also kept away fleas.

Woolen blanket

A ROOM WITHIN A ROOM
Better-off people slept in beds made from strong wooden beams with a canopy overhead and curtains at the sides. The rich may have had feather-filled mattresses, but most people's were made of straw. When the curtains were drawn, the bed became a snug, private space. This bed would have belonged to a bailiff (p. 15) in the late 15th or early 16th century.

"Truckle" bed can be wheeled out for children, servants, and others to sleep on

From kitchen to table

PEOPLE'S DIETS in the Middle Ages varied according to their means. Rich noblemen and merchants could afford to eat a wide range of food (p. 20) including expensive dried fruits, almonds, and spices from Asia. Although one poet believed the poor should live on "nettles, reeds, briars, and peashells," their diet was generally better than that. Ordinary people ate dark, coarse bread made from wheat mixed with rye or oatmeal, garden vegetables, and meat, especially pork, from their livestock. During the winter, they had to make do with meat and fish that had been preserved in salt, and cooks devised clever ways of masking the taste by adding oatmeal, peas, beans, or bread crumbs to the pot. Cows, sheep, and goats provided milk for dairy foods, which were known as "white meats."

Small pot-hanger

Adjustable ratchet

Large pot-hook for a huge cauldron

Flesh-hook for removing meat from a boiling cauldron

Fresh river trout

HOOKS FOR COOKS
Most people boiled their food in iron pots that either hung from hooks over the fire or stood in the hot ashes. Once cooked, chunks of meat were pulled out of the pot with a flesh-hook. Vegetables and grains were added to the leftover liquid to make a soupy "pottage," which was a staple part of everyone's diet. This could be turned into a thick pudding called frumenty by mixing it with wheat, crushed almonds, and egg yolks.

Pot-hook is suspended from an adjustable pot-hanger to allow the cauldron to be raised or lowered into the fire

FAST FOOD
The Church ordered that Wednesdays, Fridays, and Saturdays were "fast" days, when no meat should be eaten. Fish was allowed, and it became a vital part of the diet. Ordinary people ate mainly salted or pickled herring, fresh eels, and shellfish. The wealthy could eat carp and pike from their fishponds and a wide variety of river and sea fish.

Firewood

Pot stand, or trivet

Stone hearth

Three-legged cauldron can stand in the fire or hang from a pot-hook

Rabbits, or coneys, were a common source of fresh meat for ordinary people

A goose was often fattened for a special occasion

Wood pigeons could be wrapped in clay and baked in hot ashes

HEAD COOK

In a peasant household, the wife prepared the family's food, simmering pottage on the fire and baking bread on a hot stone. In manor or castle kitchens, the head cooks were always men. They roasted, broiled, and baked vast quantities of food in great fireplaces and ovens. A small army of kitchen boys, or scullions, were responsible for doing the clean-up.

Meat being prepared on a cutting board

IN THE PANTRY

Flesh pantries were hung with all kinds of birds and beasts. Besides mutton, beef, and pork, there was rabbit, duck, pigeon, venison, and wild boar. No bird was safe from the hunter—everything, from swans and herons to blackbirds and greenfinches, was caught for the kitchen.

Rosemary

Sage

Parsley

Mint

A HANDFUL OF HERBS

Flavoring herbs were widely used in the Middle Ages to give interesting tastes to food that was often dull or salty. Vegetables such as turnips, leeks, onions, and cabbages were also known as "pot-herbs." Not regarded as food in their own right, they were thrown into the pot to fill out soups and stews.

"Fire dogs" support the blazing logs

Fork and poker for tending fire

Kindling

ON THE HEARTH

Wattle-and-daub peasant cottages (p. 11) had no chimneys, so cooking was done on a simple stone hearth in the center of the room. Great castles and manor houses had much bigger fireplaces with huge stone chimneys where meat could be roasted on spits. The fires in the kitchens of England's King John (1167–1216) were large enough to roast two whole oxen at the same time. Since they posed a serious fire hazard, kitchens were housed in separate buildings away from the main hall.

Curfew (from the French couvre le feu) to cover the embers at night

Continued on next page

High table, low table

Dinner was the grandest and biggest meal of the day. The lord of the manor sat with his most important guests at the high table, raised on a platform, or dais, at one end of the great hall. From here, he could look down on the lesser diners and members of his household sitting at the low tables. A feast might have three courses of cooked meats and fish, elaborate roasts of swans and peacocks re-clothed in their skins, followed by numerous sweet and spicy dishes. All of these were quickly carried from the nearby kitchen so that they arrived piping hot. The lord was served first, after a sample of the food had been tasted by a servant to make sure it was not poisoned. Only then were the other diners served.

Drinking vessel

Personal knife engraved with owner's initials

Square pewter trencher base used as a personal cutting board

Spoon was provided by the house

Wooden bowl for pottage

GET SET
In the Middle Ages, table forks were rare, but everyone used their own knife, a spoon, strips of bread, and their fingers to eat very politely, for table manners were important and formed part of every wealthy child's education.

ENTERTAINING IN STYLE
At the high table, the lord sat on a bench at the center with his back to the wall. Guests were seated next to him in order of importance, starting with churchmen, then noblemen, then the lord's family. Servants scurried to and fro with meats, sauces, and pitchers of wine from the bottlery. Singers and acrobats often entertained the diners between courses.

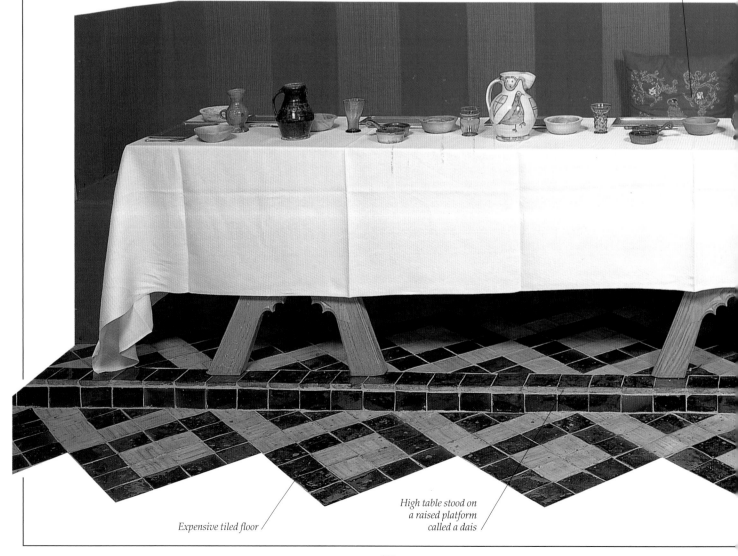

The lord's seat at the center of the table

Expensive tiled floor

High table stood on a raised platform called a dais

Large pitcher
for ale

Large wooden
platter for serving
bread or meat

Horn mug

Leather
tankard

Trestle table

*Spoons were placed face
down to "keep out the devil"*

Hard wooden bench

BANQUET BUSTLE

The banqueting hall could be a crowded,
noisy, smelly place. Tables were crammed
with diners, while dogs crunched bones
on the floor. Only the lord got a serving to
himself. Other diners shared a bowl with
up to three fellow guests. Most ate with their
fingers, so it was important that these were
clean and not used for blowing noses or
scratching. Table etiquette was strict: "If it
happens that you cannot help scratching,"
one writer advised, "then courteously take a
portion of your dress, and scratch with that."

COMMON FARE
Diners seated at a low table would have eaten less
elaborate food than that served up for the lord, but there
were some common foods. Pottage, a thick broth of vegetables
and meat stock, was a staple, everyday dish often served as
a first course at feasts. Aside from pottage, everyone ate bread. All
food was served on thick slices of stale bread called trenchers, and
small loaves called manchets were used for sopping up gravy.

Expensive
wine glass

Wooden
drinking bowl

Glazed ceramic
drinking vessel

Decorated ceramic
pitcher for wine or ale

"Double-salt" for
salt and mustard

Dyed cloth
wall-cover

*Linen tablecloth was ironed
while damp using round
glass linen smoothers*

SET FOR A LORD
The high table was carefully set out
with a clean linen tablecloth, trencher
bases, pottage and drinking bowls, salt,
pitchers, and, if the household was wealthy, fine
glasses. In the 15th century, a large communal
napkin called the long towel was spread over the
knees of the diners once they were seated.

Medieval women

"IT IS CLEAR," wrote a French priest in 1386, "that man is much nobler than woman, and of greater virtue." The medieval Church looked on women as inferior to men, and taught that they should be meek and obedient to their fathers and husbands. But the real lives of women in the Middle Ages were rather different. Not all of them stayed quietly at home, because most had to work for a living. Peasant women toiled alongside their husbands in the fields as well as having to feed and clothe their families. The wives and daughters of craftsmen were often employed in the workshop and frequently operated as tradeswomen in their own right, and wealthy ladies organized large households and sometimes ran their husbands' affairs. However, only a few powerful abbesses, noblewomen, and queens had any influence on national events.

KEEP IT COVERED
Although young single women often wore their hair loose, married women were expected to keep their hair covered in a linen "wimple" as a sign of modesty.

THE MAID OF ORLÉANS
St. Joan (c. 1412–1431) was a French peasant's daughter who, at the age of 13, heard voices telling her to drive the invading English army out of France. Dressed in armor, she led the French troops to a great victory at the besieged town of Orléans. However, Joan was later betrayed and sold to the English, who burned her as a witch.

GET THEE TO A NUNNERY
Many unmarried gentlewomen entered convents and nunneries, where they lived lives similar to those of monks (pp. 36–39). Nunneries offered women the opportunity to lead a devout life and also to obtain an education and take on responsibilities denied them in the outside world. As local landowners and employers, many abbesses were important figures in the community (above).

HOLDING THE FORT
This noblewoman has collapsed on hearing of her husband's death. Many women took on the responsibility of running large estates when their husbands died in battle or were away at court or on a crusade (p. 28). They settled local disputes, managed the farms, and handled finances. Some women even fought battles, defending their castles when they were under siege.

WOMEN OF WEALTH
Landowners, male or female, were powerful figures in medieval society, and an unmarried woman of property had equal legal rights with men. She could make a will, and sign documents with her own seal—this 13th-century seal belonged to a French noblewoman named Elizabeth of Sevorc. However, when a woman married, she forfeited her land and rights to her husband. On his death, she was entitled to a third of his land, with which to support herself.

SPINSTERS
Spinning was done almost entirely by women using handheld spindles like this one (the spinning wheel was introduced from India in the 13th century). Many single women earned a living in this way, hence the term "spinster" for an unmarried woman.

Wool twists into thread as the spindle twirls

WRAP UP
Most women covered their hair with white linen head-wraps, but the wealthy wore gold nets over their coiled braids. The well-known pointed hat called the hennin was only popular for a short time in the late 15th century.

Linen head-wrap keeps hair clean as well as hidden

Decorated hair pins

Linen shift

Prayer beads

Pin-on sleeves worn on Sundays and special occasions

AN EARLY FEMINIST
Christine de Pisan (c. 1364–1429) was one of the few medieval women to earn a living by writing. She wrote poetry and books protesting at the way women were both glorified and insulted by male authors.

THE TOWNSWOMAN
A middle-class townswoman might have worn these clothes in the 15th century. In the towns, women worked in a variety of occupations. They might be shopkeepers, spinners, bakers, or "alewives" who brewed ale. Both married and unmarried women worked for a living, often combining two or more jobs because they were paid less than men.

Woolen "kirtle" fits closely around the upper body

Leather purse serves as a pocket

Leather garters to hold up stockings

Woolen, over-the-knee stockings

Wooden "pattens" worn under shoes when muddy

Buckled leather shoes with thin soles

The great barons

Every nobleman was a vassal (p. 8) who had promised to serve his king. But many nobles grew so powerful that kings could not control them. By the 12th century, the strongest barons ruled what were really tiny, self-contained states with their own laws. The finery of their castle-courts often rivaled that of the king's, and many kept permanent armies at their beck and call. One French baron, the Sire de Coucy, had a bodyguard of 50 knights, each with 10 followers. These small private armies sometimes rode out to plunder their neighbors in savage and pitiless raids, and they posed a serious threat to the king if he did not keep his barons happy.

PARLIAMENTARY PIONEER
The English king usually governed through a Great Council of barons and churchmen. But Simon de Montfort (c. 1208–1265) wanted to limit the powers of Henry III (1207–1272). He led a rebellion in 1264, took the king prisoner, and summoned the first parliament. This was made up of the old Council, plus two representatives from each shire and town.

HIT MEN
Barons sometimes hired mercenary troops to do their fighting for them. These were bands of up to 3,000 soldiers of all nationalities— deserters from the Crusades, outlaws, and exiled knights.

VLAD DRACUL
Most infamous of all barons was the ghoulish Vlad Tepes of Romania (c. 1430–1476). According to legend, he put thousands of people to death by impaling them on stakes. He was nicknamed "Dracula," or "Dragon's son".

RALLY AROUND THE FLAG
Every nobleman had a banner such as this showing his own colors and emblems. Such flags were important rallying points for soldiers and knights on the battlefield.

Composite 15th-century flag

THE BOAST OF HERALDRY
When knights rode into battle, their faces were hidden behind armor, so they identified themselves by carrying a coat of arms, or device, on their shield. By the 13th century, these devices were used not just by warriors, but by powerful baronial families

WARLORD

Charging full-tilt at a band of helpless civilians, a fully armored knight, with his face hidden behind a great helmet, was a chilling sight. Describing an attack by the men of a great baron on the town of Durham, England, in 1143, a monk recounted: "All that came in their way was destroyed; men were hung from the walls of their own houses; others they plunged into the bed of the river; everywhere throughout the town there were groans and all kinds of deaths."

14th-century visored basinet

THE GREAT CHARTER

In June 1215, the English barons forced King John (c. 1167–1216) to sign the Magna Carta (Great Charter). This document limited the king's rights to tax the barons and to punish any man without a proper trial. But the Magna Carta did not recommend equal rights for all—ordinary people were scarcely mentioned. However, it was a crucial moment, the first time an English king had come under the control of the law.

King John's Great Seal

Wheel pommel

German battle ax, late 15th century

Single-handed French sword, 14th century

Italian war hammer, late 15th century

Fortified gatehouse, Carcassonne, France

FORTIFIED TOWNS

To protect themselves in times of war, medieval people built fortifications. The strong stone walls of castles could be seen all over the countryside, and most towns were also protected with walls, towers, and gatehouses. Some of these fortifications were massive, and the walls could be as much as 30 ft (10 m) thick. The town of Carcassonne, France, still has 54 towers and medieval walls that enclose the whole town.

MORTAL COMBAT

The baron sat as judge in his own law court. If he could not reach a clear decision, he might allow a trial by combat. Accused and accuser would put on armor and fight each other with sword and ax—whoever won the battle, won the case. Most people preferred to hire champions to fight for them. But this was not a popular line of work. The loser might be suspected of surrendering on purpose, and have his hand chopped off as a punishment!

Double-edged blade with numerous battle-scars

The royal court

THE ROYAL COURT WAS THE CENTER and the showpiece of the kingdom. Here a monarch demonstrated his power with grand ceremonies and banquets, collected taxes, settled disputes, and made laws. It was particularly important to maintain control over the powerful barons. Henry II of England (1133–1189) held special court sessions to sort out arguments over land, and Louis IX of France (1214–1270) insisted on listening to cases in person. Other monarchs amazed their subjects and visitors alike with the magnificence of their courts. Most astounding of all were the Sicilian castles of the Holy Roman Emperor (p. 6) Frederick II (1194–1250), which had golden floors, exotic animals, beautiful gardens, and dancing girls.

Love-heart decorated with tears

THE RIGHT TO RULE
Most medieval kings believed they had absolute power over their subjects, given to them by God. This sometimes led them to arrogant gestures—and disaster. Richard II of England (1367–1400) once sat for hours on his throne, glancing around. He merely wanted to watch his courtiers kneel when he looked at them. By 1399, Richard's despotic ways had made him so unpopular that he was deposed from his throne.

Lances measure about 13 ft (4 m)

LYRICS OF LOVE
Every court had its minstrels who sang songs about love and brave deeds, accompanying themselves on the harp or the lute (p. 44). The greatest love songs were written by the troubadours, who flourished in southern France in the 12th century. Each troubadour wrote in praise of his idealized lady love.

LANCE A LOT
To rebel against the king was equivalent to defying God, but if a king was weak or poor, his powerful barons could be troublesome (pp. 24–25). Monarchs were eager to lure their noblemen to court, where they could keep an eye on them. One great attraction was the joust, a contest of fighting skills. Here, two armored knights cantered toward each other, their lances held before them. The object was to hit your opponent on the head or chest and knock him off his horse.

Court ladies watch the tournament from the stand

Glittering shield may have been presented as a tournament prize

WAR GAMES

Pomp and ceremony were important parts of court life. The mock battle, or tourney, was a popular and spectacular way of amusing the court in the 11th century. While the king, queen, and courtiers looked on, large parties of knights charged at each other. If they were unhorsed, they went on fighting on foot. Tourneys were bloody and dangerous—during one fight at Cologne, more than 60 knights were killed.

IDLE PASTIMES

The lords and ladies of the court whiled away idle hours with indoor games such as backgammon, chess, and dice. Playing cards became popular in the 13th century.

"Tables" counter for playing a game similar to backgammon

OFFICIAL BUSINESS

The king made his wishes known through writs. His scribe's office produced hundreds of documents each year granting lands, and permission to raise armies, appoint officials, and order the payment of taxes. This writ, dated 1291, is a grant of game rights from Edward I of England (1239–1307) to one of his barons, Roger de Pilkington.

The royal seal makes the document official

A COURT OF LOVE

In the 12th century, courtly love became fashionable in royal circles. It was an artificial kind of passion, with strict rules. It had to be kept a secret, and the loved one had to be married—to someone else. Noble knights worshiped their ladies from afar, wrote long love poems, and vowed to do brave deeds for love. This parade shield shows a knight kneeling before his lady, and bears the motto: "You, or Death."

15th-century Flemish shield

The medieval soldier

Peace was rare in medieval times, especially in Europe. The Crusades against the Turks lasted for three centuries, and the Hundred Years' War between England and France dragged on from 1337 to 1453. Even when there were no major campaigns, barons and brigands raided their neighbors. In the early Middle Ages, the armored knight ruled the battlefield. He scorned the foot soldiers, who were mostly a rabble of poor, terrified, and untrained peasants pressed into battle by their lords. But by the 15th century, knights were fast going out of fashion and the common soldier became much more important. He developed into a professional warrior, well-paid, skillful with his weapon, and used to obeying orders. Many even worked as mercenary soldiers, hiring themselves out to the highest bidder.

THE CRUSAD
In 1095, the Pope called for a holy w against the Muslim rulers of Palestir called the Holy Land by Christian A European army set off on the Fir Crusade and recaptured the ho city of Jerusalem, but the Muslin soon advanced again. Another eig crusades followed between 11 and 1270, all of them failures. Th 15th-century painting shows crusade arriving at Damietta in Egy

ARCH ENEMY
Archers played a key role in the decline of the knight in the 15th century. Fired at the enemy from a safe distance, a deadly hail of arrows killed men and horses alike. Without their horses, heavily armored knights were easy prey for foot soldiers.

Glaive, a form of pole weapon used for stabbing or knocking the enemy aside; it was safer to keep opponents at arm's length

Wooden drinking bowl for ale

Pottage bowl and spoon

Canvas kit bag

Cloth-charcoal, or tinder

Steel

Flint

Flint, steel, and tinder for lighting camp fires

Chain splints keep swords from slicing through the arm

Sheepskin mitten worn inside

Mitten gauntlet protects the hand and wrist

Leather boots generally lasted about three months

FOOTSORE AND HUNGRY
Life on the march could be very hard. A foot soldier would have to walk at least 6 miles (10 km) a day, and occasionally three times as far. His food bowl was often empty, for a large army soon consumed everything edible in the surrounding countryside. Starving French soldiers in the First Crusade of 1097 were told to feed on their enemies: "Are there not corpses of Turks in plenty? Cooked and salted they will be good to eat!"

Peak
protects
the neck

Military
"bollock"
dagger

Eating
knife

Visor limits
vision, so was
lowered only
in fierce
fighting

Sallet
helmet

HANDSOME RANSOM
A captured enemy could be a valuable
acquisition. Important prisoners
were often held to ransom for
large sums of money. When
King Richard I of England
(1157–99) was captured in
1194, his country had to
pay 150,000 marks—
a huge sum.

BELT BAG
A soldier had to carry his personal
belongings with him wherever he went,
so luggage was kept to a minimum. Slung
from his belt, this leather purse probably
contained money, dice for gambling,
needles and thread, and a kerchief.

HAND-TO-HAND FIGHTING
With a sword in his right hand and
a buckler in his left, a soldier was a
dangerous enemy. The buckler was
not only used to deflect blows, but
also to hit an opponent in the face,
before jabbing or slashing
with the sword. However,
the soldier did most
of his fighting with
a pole weapon, and
relied on his sword
as a last resort.
There were no
rules of combat
in medieval
warfare, and
most battles
were terrifying
free-for-alls.

Gauntlet
limits wrist
movement

Small fist shield,
or buckler, for
punching

I'M ALRIGHT, JACK
This military outfit
would have been worn by
a professional foot soldier in
the late 15th century. Some
of his gear would have been
issued to him, and the rest
was probably stolen, or
looted. Most soldiers at
this time wore much less
armor than the knights of
old. A padded tunic called
a jack, with iron gauntlets
and arm splints, gave good
protection against sword
and dagger cuts.

Thin
leather belt

Close-fitting
canvas arming doublet

Quilted jack
made from
multilayered
canvas

Single-handed
sword for
hand-to-hand
combat

The Church

THE CHRISTIAN CHURCH was at the center of medieval life. There were two main branches in the West: the Catholic Church based in Rome, and the Orthodox Church based in Constantinople (now Istanbul). With its own laws, lands, and taxes, the Catholic Church was a powerful institution. It governed almost every aspect of people's lives, from the practical to the spiritual. Most men and women, rich and poor, were baptized and married in church and attended mass every Sunday of their lives. When they died, their priest read them the last rites, and they were buried on church ground. For many, life on Earth was hard and short, but the Church stated that if they followed the teachings of Christ, they would at least be rewarded in heaven. This idea gave the Church great power over people's hearts and minds.

LEADERS OF MEN
Archbishops were powerful men who sat on the king's council and played a leading role in government.

BIRD OF BLESSING
Suspended above the altar, this golden dove symbolized the Holy Spirit during the Eucharist—the Catholic ceremony where bread and wine are blessed and eaten to commemorate the sacrifice of Christ.

Censer is suspended on gilded chains

CHURCH TREASURES
By the 14th century, the Church had grown hugely wealthy. Money poured in from rents, tithes (p. 13), and the sale of indulgences (pardons for sins). Larger churches could afford to buy expensive sacramental vessels like this beautiful 14th-century silver chalice.

Burning incense is placed inside the censer

PARISH PRACTICES
The life of a parish priest was often a hard one. Many were poor men who lacked any serious education. Most of a priest's income came from fees charged for baptisms (above), marriages, and burial services. He also had his own land in the village, called the glebe, where he grew his own food. Aside from preaching, a village priest tended to the sick and poor, and the better-educated taught Latin and Bible stories to local boys.

SWINGING CENSERS
During mass, priests swung censers full of burning incense. People believed that if they attended mass regularly, they would be rewarded by God—and the more masses, the greater the reward. The wealthy could pay to have the "Trental," or 30 masses, said for them.

CONDEMNED TO THE FLAMES
Few people challenged the authority of the Church, but those who did were severely punished. People who disagreed with the Church's teachings were called heretics. They faced being brought to trial in a Church court and, under its special laws, could be condemned to be whipped or burned at the stake. The Cathar sect of southern France rejected the beliefs of the Catholic Church by claiming that everything on Earth was created by the devil. In 1208, the Pope ordered a crusade against them. Over the next 26 years, thousands of Cathars were tortured and burned in huge bonfires until they were completely wiped out.

ISIONS OF HELL
he Church taught that when a erson died, the good and bad deeds f their life were literally weighed in he balance by God. Their soul was ither carried to heaven by angels or ragged off to hell by demons. Hell as a real and terrifying place for eople in medieval times, and its orments were pictured in vivid etail by numerous painters.

Angel swings a golden censer

Carved wooden angels from a medieval church nave (p. 39)

Angel holds a tiny church

Picture shows the coronation of the Virgin by Christ

Angel holds a gilded casket

BISHOP'S MITER
Bishops were the local leaders of the Church. From their great cathedrals, they ruled over groups of parishes called dioceses. They usually came from noble families and were involved in affairs of state as well as those of the Church. Some were pious and learned men, but others were not—one 13th-century Italian bishop admitted that he did not believe in Christianity, and had only taken the office "because of its riches and honors."

14th-century bishop's hat, or miter

VICAR OF CHRIST
The Pope was head of the Catholic Church and represented God on Earth. This massive gilt ring belonged to Pope Eugenius IV, who was pope from 1431 to 1447.

Building a cathedral

In the early Middle Ages, large churches were built in the Romanesque style. They had massive pillars and thick walls to hold up the round-arched roofs. As a result, windows were small, and Romanesque churches were sometimes dark and gloomy. By the 12th century, they were too small for the booming population of Europe, and for the growing stream of pilgrims (pp. 42–43). There was an explosion of cathedral building, starting in 1140 with the Abbey of St. Denis near Paris. This was constructed in a startling new style, called Gothic, where the weight of the roof rested not on the walls, but on outside supports called buttresses. This allowed walls to be thinner, and pierced with tall windows that led the eye heavenward and flooded the cathedral with light.

SYMPHONIES IN STONE
Before 1350, 80 cathedrals were built in France alone. Among the first to use flying buttresses was Reims Cathedral, begun in 1211.

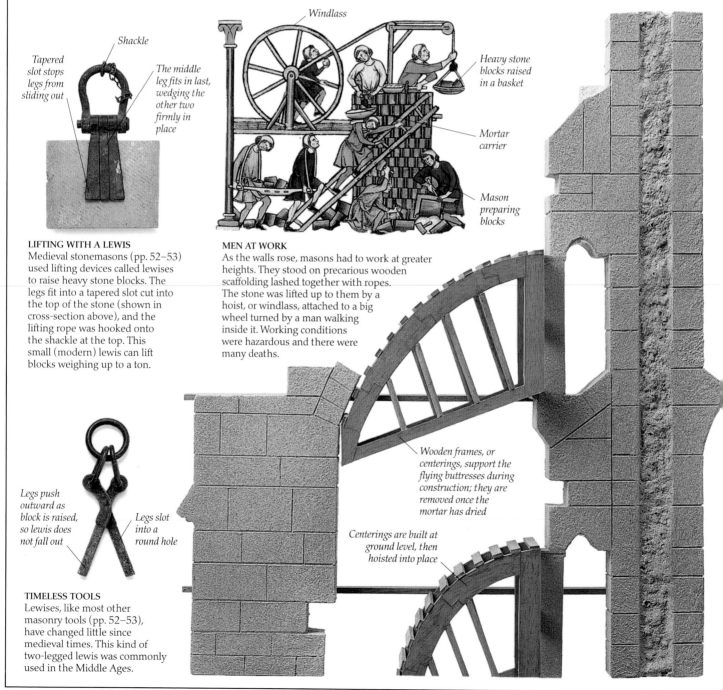

Shackle

Tapered slot stops legs from sliding out

The middle leg fits in last, wedging the other two firmly in place

Windlass

Heavy stone blocks raised in a basket

Mortar carrier

Mason preparing blocks

LIFTING WITH A LEWIS
Medieval stonemasons (pp. 52–53) used lifting devices called lewises to raise heavy stone blocks. The legs fit into a tapered slot cut into the top of the stone (shown in cross-section above), and the lifting rope was hooked onto the shackle at the top. This small (modern) lewis can lift blocks weighing up to a ton.

MEN AT WORK
As the walls rose, masons had to work at greater heights. They stood on precarious wooden scaffolding lashed together with ropes. The stone was lifted up to them by a hoist, or windlass, attached to a big wheel turned by a man walking inside it. Working conditions were hazardous and there were many deaths.

Legs push outward as block is raised, so lewis does not fall out

Legs slot into a round hole

Wooden frames, or centerings, support the flying buttresses during construction; they are removed once the mortar has dried

Centerings are built at ground level, then hoisted into place

TIMELESS TOOLS
Lewises, like most other masonry tools (pp. 52–53), have changed little since medieval times. This kind of two-legged lewis was commonly used in the Middle Ages.

SOARING TO THE SKY
Gothic cathedrals were held up by skeletons of stone. The ribs were in the vaulted ceilings, which supported the massive stone-tiled roofs. These ribs of delicate stone rested on pillars and curved up to meet in a junction with a pointed arch. The spaces, or vaults, between the ribs were filled with a course of smaller stones. This method of building was so strong and light that cathedrals could be made higher than ever before. Throughout the 12th and 13th centuries, they soared up and up—the choir roof at Beauvais, France, reached a staggering 157 ft (48 m)!

LET THERE BE LIGHT
The tall, vertical lines of this 15th-century window draw the eye upward, which is why this English late Gothic style is called Perpendicular. Delicately carved stone tracery (p. 53) supported vast panels of vivid stained glass (pp. 34–35).

FLYING FORCE
The other vital bones of a Gothic cathedral's skeleton were the buttresses. Stone roofs were so heavy that they pressed down the ribbed vaults onto the pillars and forced them outward. To counteract this, huge buttresses were built onto the outside, pushing inward. However, buttresses could not bear all the weight, especially at the top, where the ribs met the walls. Here, extra "flying" buttresses curved across the vault, transferring the outward thrust downward.

Space between blocks is filled with rubble

Gutter

Flying buttress reinforces the wall

Spout

EARLY EXAMPLE
The elaborate styles of High Gothic windows evolved from simple, 13th-century lancets like these.

SPITTING IMAGES
Rainwater was drained off the roof into the gutters, and then shot out, well clear of the walls, through spouts. These spouts were often carved into gargoyles—grotesque faces that appeared to be spitting water.

The art of decoration

"I AM A POOR OLD WOMAN WHO KNOWS NOTHING, who cannot read. But in the Church I see Paradise painted, and Hell where the damned broil." These were the words of a 15th-century French woman, and they spoke for millions of uneducated people in medieval Europe. For them, cathedrals and churches were not just places of worship, they were picture books and art galleries. The great cathedrals were filled with statues and carvings, painted panels and frescoes, which told stories of saints and biblical characters. Most wonderful of all were the stained glass windows through which light streamed in dazzling, brilliant colors.

ICONS FROM THE EAST
The inspiration for Europe's church decorators came from the glittering Eastern city of Byzantium (modern-day Istanbul). This sacred picture, or icon, of Christ glows with gold and rich colors. Icons were revered as holy objects.

Line of sketch, o cartoon

Soldered joint

Hog's-hair scrub

Stippler for scraping away highlights once a color wash has been applied

Tracing brush for applying fine lines

Latherkin for smoothing out the lead

Groziers for snipping bits off a glass shape; flint was used in medieval times

Modern glaziers' tools

GLAZIERS AND GROZIERS
Most glass came to the glass painters, or glaziers, from countryside kilns. It was already colored, and the glaziers cut and shaped the glass pieces. They could vary the colors by scraping away the surface or by painting it with enamels.

THE WHOLE PICTURE
Like a fragile and beautiful jigsaw puzzle, the stained glass pieces fit together with the lead. The glass slots into grooves in each side of the lead strips, and the whole assembly is held firm with large horseshoe nails. Finally, the joints between the strips are soldered back and front, and putty is applied to seal in the glass. The completed panel is then set with others into the delicate stone tracery (p. 53) of a window. The lead will last for over 100 years before it needs to be replaced.

34

Wicked devil urges on the three gossips

Line of clear glass is known as the white, or sacrificial, line, because it was most likely to be broken when the panel was removed for releading

Cut and painted glass shape

STORIES IN GLASS
Stained glass windows were like religious cartoons. Through pictures, they taught religious lessons and the stories of the Bible to those who could not read. This panel depicts three gossiping women with leering devils at their shoulders. The moral is clear—don't speak badly about others!

CUT AND COLORED
In medieval times, the design for a window was drawn onto a board coated with chalk and water. Glass pieces were placed over the design and cut to shape, using a hot iron to score the glass. Final trimming was done by nibbling the edges with a grozier. The details of the picture were painted on with enamel, then the glass was fired to fuse in the paint.

Space left for lead is known as the "cut line"

The lead has grooves along each side, into which the glass fits

Charlemagne was a renowned Christian king

BEAUTIFUL BLUE
Medieval glassmakers produced primary colors by adding metallic oxides to the molten glass. The glowing colors they created were named after precious stones—ruby red, emerald green, and sapphire blue. The recipes for different colors were closely guarded secrets, and most have since been lost. The beautiful blue glass in these famous windows at Chartres Cathedral, France, was known as *bleu de ciel*—"heavenly blue."

Large nails hold the jigsaw of glass and lead together before soldering

Lead is soft and can be shaped around the glass quite easily

A SHINING EXAMPLE
Altarpieces usually portrayed great moments from the story of Christ. This altar panel was painted in 1333 for Siena Cathedral, Italy, by Simone Martini and Lippo Memmi. It shows the Archangel Gabriel announcing to Mary that she will bear the baby Jesus. The style is much more natural than the stiff and formal design of Byzantine icons. The central figures, glowing against a golden background, are full of graceful movement.

An altarpiece is set behind the altar

Holy orders

"WE MUST FORM A SCHOOL IN THE LORD'S SERVICE," wrote St. Benedict in the sixth century. He founded a monastery at Monte Cassino in Italy where monks could live, work, and pray together. The monks became known as the Benedictines because they followed St. Benedict's "Rule," which instructed them to make three vows—of poverty (to own no property), chastity (never to marry), and obedience (to obey the orders of their leaders). Making these vows was a serious undertaking, so St. Benedict ordered that every newcomer, or novice, should live in the monastery for a year before committing himself. Once he had made his vows, a novice had the crown of his head shaved in a tonsure, and he became a brother of the order. In time, monasteries and convents throughout Europe adopted St. Benedict's Rule.

12th-century Celtic monk

Bone stylus

Wax tablet on a horn base

WAX COPY BOOK
Monks spent a lot of time copying out prayers and psalms by hand. They often wrote on wax tablets with a scratcher, or stylus. Copying holy passages was also a way of serving God. St. Bernard (1090–1153) told monks: "Every word you write is a blow that smites the devil."

Tonsure

THE HISTORY MAN
Many monks were well educated, and monasteries became centers of learning. St. Bede (c. 673–735), also known as the Venerable Bede, was an English Benedictine monk who devoted his life to writing and scholarship. He wrote books on science, religion, and history, including the great *Ecclesiastical History of the English Nation*. Without monks like Bede, we would know much less about the history of the Middle Ages.

NO LIGHT IN THE DARKNESS
St. Benedict's Rule allowed for basic comforts, but life in a monastery was never easy. At first, monks were not allowed candles for reading at services—they had to learn all the prayers, psalms, and other forms of worship by heart.

OUT OF ORDER
By the 10th century, many religious houses had become too relaxed. The monk below has been placed in the stocks with his mistress as a punishment for an illicit affair. Some French monks thought that the ideals of St. Benedict were being forgotten and formed a new order at Cluny in 910. The Cluniacs tried to follow the strict and simple rules laid down by St. Benedict. Other new orders were the Carthusians, who believed in a life of silent prayer, and the Cistercians, who thought that hard work was the best way to serve God.

THE FRANCISCANS
St. Francis of Assisi (c. 1182–1226) was the son of a rich man, yet he gave away all his possessions to live like one of Christ's disciples. He founded a new order of holy brothers in Italy, called Franciscan friars. Instead of living in monasteries, they took the word of God to the people, traveling around preaching and begging for their food. An order of Franciscan nuns was founded by one of St. Francis's followers named St. Clare.

Plain rope belt

Bare feet

Linen shift worn underneath the habit

Warm cloak worn in cold weather

Long woolen habit was supposed to emulate Roman clothing

Simple, hand-sewn leather shoes; Benedictines did not have to wear sandals

HEAD WARMER
In winter, chilly drafts whistled through the stone corridors and bare cells of a monastery. Only the sick room was always heated. Although the monastic way of life was often harsh, St. Benedict did not believe that monks should sacrifice their health in the service of God. His Rule stated that a monk's clothes should be plain but comfortable, and Benedictines were allowed to wear linen coifs such as this one to keep their heads warm. The Cistercians rejected such soft ways. Many of them went barefoot, and some even wore hairy underclothes as a sign of devotion to God.

Wooden-bead rosary, or paternoster, for counting prayers

Eating knife

Benedictines were allowed to wear leather belts

HABIT OF A LIFETIME
The oldest and largest of the monastic orders, the Benedictines were known as the Black Monks because of the color of their habits. Each of the new orders formed in the 10th, 11th, and 12th centuries had its own distinguishing dress. For example, the Cistercians wore rough tunics of undyed wool and became known as the White Monks. Nevertheless, the basic style of the habit has remained the same to this day.

Life in a monastery

MONASTERIES AND CONVENTS were worlds of their own. Ruled by an abbot or an abbess, they were cut off from society and governed by special rules. When novices (p. 36) entered a holy order, they were expected to stay there for the rest of their lives. From that moment on, every part of each day was accounted for. Much of the time was spent attending the eight daily church services and reading or copying religious texts. Other duties included caring for the poor and sick, teaching younger members of the order, or tending to the gardens, fish ponds, mill, and farm. There was a general rule of silence in most religious houses, and daily tasks had to be carried out without speaking. Although they lived apart from society, monks and nuns served an important role in the community. They provided food for the poor, care for the sick, and accommodation for pilgrims and other travelers.

ROUND OF PRAYERS
Monks went to the monastery church eight times a day in an unchanging round of services, or offices. The first, Matins, began at two o'clock in the morning, and dormitories were built near the church so that the monks wouldn't be late for services. In the early 11th century, monks at Canterbury, England, had to sing 55 psalms, one after the other, and all without sitting down. The Benedictines shown here at least have pews to rest on.

Single-chambered wicker beehive daubed with clay

Straw hackle, or jacket, placed over the hive in winter to keep the bees warm

Statue of Mary and Jesus

Wicker beehive made from woven willow or hazel

Abbey church

Model of an abbey in the 15th century

BUSY BEES
The Cistercians (p. 36) believed that performing hard manual labor was the best way to lead a holy life. They built large monasteries in remote rural areas where they could farm the land in peace. Their estates grew so big that lay brothers (those who had taken holy vows but lacked the education to become monks) were taken on to help. Most monasteries had to produce their own food. These beehives, or skeps, provided honey to eat and wax for candles.

CARE IN A CONVENT
Nuns took the same vows as monks (p. 36) and lived in much the same way. Devoted to serving the poor, most convents and monasteries ran hospitals to care for the sick. These were open to all, and nuns and monks were instructed: "Receive the patients as you would Christ Himself." The medicines and treatments may have been primitive (pp. 60–61), but at least patients were given food and a clean bed. Without the work of the Church, there would have been very little health care in the Middle Ages.

A GREAT MONASTERY
The layouts of monasteries followed a standardized pattern from the ninth century onward, except for Carthusian (p. 36) monasteries, where the monks lived in individual cells. This 12th-century ground-plan of Canterbury Cathedral and monastery shows how nearly everything the monks needed was contained within the walls. The main building was the church, the largest and grandest they could afford. On the sunny south side lay the cloister, a covered walkway surrounding an open square sheltered from the wind. This was the center of community life where the monks might stroll, sit, or read. Another meeting place was the chapter house where the abbot held assemblies to discuss important matters.

Cathedral

Main cloister

Water tower

Herbarium

Infirmary

The latrines, or necessarium

Dormitory

Refectory

Kitchens

Chapter house

Bell tower

Nave

Transept

Cloister

Dormitory

Refectory

Main entrance

Undercroft or storage rooms

AN AUGUSTINIAN ABBEY
This small abbey housed an order of Augustinian canons. Formed in the 12th century, they followed the Rule of St. Augustine, which allowed them to live as monks but also perform clerical duties in churches and cathedrals.

Abbot's lodge

The written word

Uɴᴛɪʟ 1200, ʙᴏᴏᴋs ᴡᴇʀᴇ ʀᴀʀᴇ and were usually found only in monastery libraries. Everything was written by hand and monks spent many hours in the "scriptorium" copying out religious texts. A long manuscript such as the Bible might take one scribe a year to complete. As a way of glorifying God, many manuscripts were beautifully decorated, or illuminated, with jewel-like paints and precious gold leaf. After 1200, books became more common, especially when the first universities opened in Paris and Bologna. Professional scribes and illuminators began to produce books as well as the monks, often making copies to order for wealthy customers. Personal books of psalms, called psalters, became popular among the aristocracy.

1 GESSO WORK
One of the most striking features of medieval manuscripts are the beautifully decorated capital letters that begin each page. Painted in vibrant colors, they were often gilded with gold leaf to make them even brighter. The first stage of illuminating a letter is applying the gesso, a kind of glue made from plaster, white lead, water, sugar, and egg white. The gesso makes a sticky surface for the gold.

The gold leaf sticks only to the moist gesso

The molded gesso gives a 3-D effect to the gilded leaves

Each leaf burnish separate

3 BURNISHED BRIGHT
Once the gold leaf has set into the gesso, the illuminator rubs, or burnishes, it to make it shiny. The traditional burnishing tool was a dog's or wolf's tooth attached to a wooden handle. Finally, the rest of the background is carefully painted in around the gilding.

2 GILDING THE LETTER
The gesso is left to set over night, and the next day the illuminator smooths any rough edges and breathes on the gesso to make it slightly moist. He then lays a sheet of gold leaf over the gesso, covers it with a silk cloth and presses it firmly onto the glue. The surplus gold is removed with a soft brush.

SCRIBES AND SCHOLARS
However hard scribes worked, books remained scarce. Few people could afford to buy them, and scholars had to travel around monastic libraries to study the texts they wanted. This statue of a scholar is from Chartres Cathedral, France.

4 SHINING THROUGH THE AGES
The finished letter is like a tiny work of art. Aside from leaves and flowers, many illuminated initials contain pictures of people and animals. If the gold is properly burnished it will never fade— most medieval manuscripts still shine brightly today.

Curling leaves are a popular Gothic design

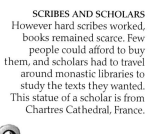

Bone spectacles

SIGHT FOR SORE EYES
Hours of close copying required sharp eyesight. Europeans first started wearing eyeglasses in the 13th century. The invention of printing in the 1450s (p. 62) made more books available, and the sale of eyeglasses skyrocketed.

Feather is rarely left on the quill because it gets in the way

A LITTLE LEARNING
Most schooling in the Middle Ages took place in monasteries, convents, and cathedrals. Children (mostly boys who were destined for holy orders) received a basic education in reading and writing, and spent much of their time learning prayers and Bible passages by heart—all in Latin. They were often forbidden to talk or play and were beaten with a birch rod when their attention wandered!

THE PROPHET'S BOOK
Muslims believe the Qu'ran is the word of God revealed to the Prophet Muhammad. At first it was not written down, but memorized by his followers. After Muhammad's death in 632 CE, the first written texts were produced. Throughout the Middle Ages, scribes created many beautiful editions of the Qu'ran, richly decorated with geometric patterns.

Point used for pricking outlines on parchment

Stylus   Goose quills

Inkwell slots into a hole in the desk

Horn inkwells

Selection of quills

Sloping desk

Drinking vessel

Straight-backed chair made from white ash wood

Pitcher of ale or weak wine for refreshment

Horn books to copy from

Tabletop folds backward

SEAT FOR A SCRIBE
A scribe might sit for hours at his work copying out Latin texts in beautiful, well-formed script. He rested his parchment on a sloping desk, which made it easier to hold his pen at right angles (quills wrote best this way). In his left hand, he held a pen-knife, which he used to hold down the page, to scrape out mistakes, and to sharpen his quill—often up to 60 times a day.

Cushion made long hours of work more comfortable

Folding table, or tabula plicata, can be stored flat against a wall

Decoration carved only on the side that faces the room

Chair leg decorated with bands of vermilion paint

Saints and pilgrims

Most people in the Middle Ages hoped to go on a pilgrimage to a holy shrine at some point in their lives. They went for many reasons—as proof of their devotion to God, as an act of penance for their sins, or to find a cure for an illness. The holy city of Jerusalem was a favorite destination, as were Rome, where both St. Peter and St. Paul were believed to be buried, the shrine of St. James at Santiago de Compostela in Spain, and Canterbury Cathedral in England. On the road, rich and poor traveled together and, for many, pilgrimages were a sort of vacation. To pass the time, people sang songs and hymns, played pipes, and told stories over their evening meals in roadside taverns.

ON THE ROAD
In the early Middle Ages, most pilgrims traveled on foot. They wore broad-brimmed felt hats, long woolen tunics, called sclaveins, and sandals.

Scallop shell emblem of Santiago de Compostela

SIGN OF THE SHRINE
Like modern tourists, medieval pilgrims often sported pins to show that they had been to a certain shrine. They wore them on their hats to make it clear that they were on a holy journey and had the right to protection. The scallop shell was a popular emblem.

Front part of reliquary contains a holy cross set in pearls and rock crystal

Tiny flask, or ampulla, for holy water

Pewter badge of St. Thomas Becket

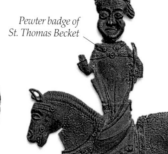

PORTABLE RELICS
Holy relics, or the bones of saints, were not only kept in shrines. People carried them in bags around their necks or in beautifully decorated cases like this one. Knights often had relics placed in their sword hilts.

Back part of reliquary contains pieces of bone, or relics, set in gold as a sign of their value

Figure of Christ

A MARTYR'S BONES
This 12th-century reliquary casket depicts the murder of Archbishop Thomas Becket (1118–1170), on Henry II's orders, in Canterbury Cathedral in 1170. Becket became a saint and Canterbury, resting place of his bones, quickly became a place of pilgrimage.

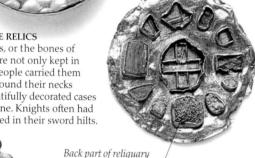

Becket's body is laid in a shroud

Becket is carried to heaven by angels

One of the king's knights slices off Becket's head

THE PILGRIM'S POET
Geoffrey Chaucer (c. 1340–1400) wrote the best-loved book about pilgrims, *The Canterbury Tales*. It is a series of stories in verse told by a party of 30 pilgrims to pass the time as they ride to Canterbury. The pilgrims, who include a knight, a miller, a friar, a prioress, and a cook, portray a vivid and often hilarious picture of medieval life.

Crown of semiprecious stones

INSIDE STORY
This wooden head fits inside the large gold head and was the real receptacle for the relics of St. Eustace.

Wealthy pilgrims on horseback

PILGRIM'S PROGRESS
Robbers and brigands were a constant threat to the medieval traveler, so pilgrims journeyed together in groups for safety, sometimes even taking an armed escort. On popular routes, such as the one to Santiago de Compostela in Spain, local rulers built special roads and bridges, and monks set up hostels, spaced a day's journey apart.

Head is made of silver gilded with gold

HOLY HEAD
A reliquary was a special casket for holding relics, such as the bones of a saint or a splinter of Christ's cross. Relics were displayed in shrines where they were visited by pilgrims. People believed they had almost magical powers, such as the power to cure diseases or bring victory in battle. This beautiful, 13th-century gilded head contained the relics of St. Eustace, an early Christian saint, and was displayed in Basel Cathedral, Switzerland.

The Islamic world

MUHAMMAD, FOUNDER OF THE ISLAMIC RELIGION, died in 632 CE. Within 100 years, a great Islamic civilization had developed and Arab armies had conquered a vast empire that stretched from Spain and North Africa to Persia and India. International trade flourished in the Islamic world, spreading ideas as well as goods. Muslim scientists became particularly advanced in the fields of medicine and mathematics: they were skilled surgeons and eye doctors, invented algebra (from the Arabic *al-jebr*), and introduced the Arabic numeral system to Europe, a version of which is still in use today. Although the Christians saw the Muslims as an "infidel" race and an almost inhuman enemy during the Crusades, as trade links grew stronger, they learned much from this highly advanced civilization.

THE ALHAMBRA
The Muslims were finally driven out of Spain by the Christians in 1492. Their last stronghold was the palace and fortress called the Alhambra ("Red Castle") in Granada. Completed in the 14th century, it is one of the most beautiful buildings in the world, with marble colonnades, tiled walls, fountains, and pools.

Inlaid decoration

Traditional Arabic pattern

MUSLIM MARVEL
The lute almost came to symbolize medieval European music, but its true origin was in the Islamic world, where it was known as *al-'ud*. Many Muslim rulers, or caliphs, were great patrons of art and learning, and fostered the work of musicians, poets, artists, and scholars at their courts. The lute was just one of many inventions and ideas that came to Europe from the Muslim empire.

HEAVENLY GUIDANCE
The Muslims were brilliant astronomers. They developed the astrolabe, which enabled travelers to fix their position by studying the night sky. Camel drivers used this instrument to navigate across the desert. Europeans copied the idea and used astrolabes for finding their way at sea.

LUXURY TRAIN
Camel trains carried a huge range of goods across the deserts and mountains of the Islamic world. In the dazzling bazaars of Baghdad and Damascus, the wealthy could buy a stunning variety of luxury goods, from Persian carpets and African ivory to Asian silks, spices, jewels, and furs.

HERO OF A HOLY WAR
Saladin (c. 1137–1193) was a great Islamic sultan who led the Muslim armies against the crusaders and recaptured Jerusalem. He was respected even by his enemies as a brilliant general and a wise man.

MEDICINE MEN
Even as the Crusades were raging, Europeans learned a great deal from Islamic doctors, whose knowledge was far in advance of their own. Cures for numerous ills could be bought in apothecaries such as this. In the 11th century, the great Arab doctor Avicenna (c. 980–1037) wrote a medical encyclopedia that became the single greatest influence on medieval medicine.

ARTS AND CRAFTS
Islamic craftsmen were renowned for their beautiful enamel work. They usually decorated religious artifacts, such as this 13th-century mosque lamp, with Arabic words and geometric patterns. This was because Islamic tradition banned images of human figures and other living things from religious buildings.

Trade and commerce

THE EARLIEST MEDIEVAL MERCHANTS were peddlers who sold goods to villages and towns. By the 12th century, Europe had grown more prosperous and more goods were produced. Merchants were no longer simply wandering adventurers. They became dealers, employers, and ship owners, sending their carriers along a network of trade routes linking the European cities. By 1300, cargo ships from Genoa and Venice in Italy were taking precious metals, silks, and other luxuries from the eastern Mediterranean out to England and Flanders (Belgium). There they picked up wool, coal, and lumber for the return voyage. German and Dutch ships took iron, copper, and lead south to the Mediterranean, and brought back wine, oil, and salt.

Quills were trimmed before use

One half of a tally stick

CANDLE WAX
This tiny candle was used to melt the wax for sealing letters and documents.

BALANCING THE BOOKS
Merchants needed to keep careful accounts of their money. Traders in 14th-century Florence developed a system of double-entry bookkeeping. Each deal was recorded in two ledgers—one for credits, the other for debits. The amounts in each ledger should always balance.

Horn inkwell and quill

TALLY STICK
A debt could be recorded on a tally stick. Notches were cut into it to record the amount, then the stick was split in two and each party kept half. When the debt was settled, the tally was destroyed or kept as a record.

KEEP THE CHANGE
Merchants kept small numbers of coins in money boxes like this. Most coins were silver, but in 1252, the city of Florence minted the first gold coins since Roman times— the golden florin.

14th-century document seal

SIGNED AND SEALED
As trading methods grew more complex, much more paperwork was needed. Merchants had to employ clerks and scribes to help them. There were letters giving details of business deals, bills of sale, orders, contracts to suppliers, and documents promising payment. All of these had to be signed and marked with the wax seals of the merchants involved.

Late-medieval
purse frame

For most of the Middle Ages, paper
was scarce and few people could read
or write, so traders added up their
cash on a counter board marked out
with columns. Counters, or jettons,
were added to a column until
they reached a certain total
(usually 10). Then they
were removed, and
counting began in
the next column.

THE HANSEATIC LEAGUE
In the 13th century, trading towns on
the North Sea and Baltic coasts, including
Hamburg (above), united to form the
Hanseatic League. Their goal was
to help each other in fighting
pirates and bandits, and to
gain exclusive control of
foreign trade. The League
grew very powerful—
by 1400, it had offices
in 160 towns
in northern
Europe.

Silver deniers and purse

WEIGHING IT UP
Most medieval
merchants carried
small coin balances for
weighing different currencies
to determine their value.

Tumbrel coin
balance

*Spike sticks
into desktop*

14th-century
keys for locking
away valuables

MONEY MEN
Banking began
in Italy with
moneylenders who
did business on benches,
or *banchi*. They grew rich
on the interest they charged
for their services. The cities of
Florence, Venice, Siena, and Genoa
became particularly prosperous.
However, the business was not without its
hazards—two wealthy banks in Florence were
ruined in the 1350s when Edward III of England
(1312–1377) was unable to repay a massive loan.

Life in the town

As TRADE GREW, so did towns. At first they were part of a lord's or king's domain, but as they became wealthier, townsmen resented having to work for someone else. In northern France, there were violent scenes as towns struggled to become independent "communes." In England, the process was more peaceful. Town-dwellers agreed to pay a fixed sum each year in return for a royal charter that granted them the right to govern themselves. The town then became a free "borough" with the power to make its own laws, form trade guilds (p. 50), and raise taxes. The people also became free citizens, or burgesses.

THE NIGHT WATCH
At sunset, the town bells rang to sound the curfew. This meant that everyone had to finish work and go home. There were no street lights in medieval towns, and they could be dangerous places after dark. Nightwatchmen patrolled the streets with lanterns to deter criminals.

STREET SIGN
Towns were first and foremost centers o trade with bustling streets full of shop Since few people could read, many shop advertised their wares by hanging out symbol of their trade, such as a loaf for baker or a basin for a barber (seen in th middle of the picture). In some town traders or craftsmen of the same type ha shops in the same street, so shoemake worked in Shoe Lane, tailors o Threadneedle Street, fishmongers the Rue de la Poissonerie, and so o

15th-century French city

WALLED IN
Medieval towns were surrounded by strong stone walls. These were not only to keep out villains. They also made sure that merchants and other visitors could only enter by the gates, where they had to pay a toll. Town gates were opened at dawn and locked at dusk.

THE LORD MAYOR
Most towns were governed by an elected mayor and a local council. Mayors became powerful figures who were often courted by lords and kings. Some even loaned money to the monarch. Dick Whittington (c. 1358–1423) was a famous English mayor. The son of a knight, he became a wealthy merchant and was elected Lord Mayor of London three times.

TOWERS THAT BE
Powerful families struggled to gain control of the new communes and boroughs. In Italy, they built defensive towers as symbols of their wealth and importance. At San Gimignano in Tuscany, over 70 towers were erected in the 12th century. Eventually, most town councils forbade any building higher than the town hall!

GARDEY LOO!
Slop pails and chamber pots were emptied out of windows with the cry "Gardey loo!" from the French *gardez l'eau*, which means "Look out, water!" Town-dwellers were naturally wary when walking down the street!

"Half-moon" leather knife

Spike possibly used to make holes for stitching

Hooklike leather knife

LIVING OVER THE SHOP
Most craftsmen had their workshops on the ground floors of their homes. These also served as shops, and finished goods were displayed on a hinged shelf at the front. In the evening, shutters were pulled down for security. The shopkeeper usually had a storeroom at the back, and he and his family lived on the floors above. This 15th-century building is divided into two shops. Only the smaller shop on the right has access to the upper floors, which means that the other was probably rented out to another business.

Upper stories were home to the shopkeeper's family

A staircase at the rear leads to the upper chambers

Sole made from tough cattle hide

Waxed linen thread

Upper made from goatskin, which is strong and flexible

Half-finished shoe will be turned other way out when complete

LEAN STREETS
There was a limited amount of space within the walls of a medieval town, and houses were built very close together. To maximize space, the upper stories of buildings were jettied, or built jutting out above the ground floors. In some places, the houses on either side almost touched each other, making some streets quite gloomy and airless.

TOWN TRADE
Craftsmen such as shoemakers worked at windows that opened onto the street, giving them the opportunity to show off their skills to passers-by. Medieval shoemakers were known as cordwainers, after the best shoe-leather from Cordoba in Spain. These long-toed "poulaine" shoes were fashionable in the late 14th century and would have been sold to a wealthy merchant or burgess.

The guild masters

In 1262, A BOOK OF TRADES compiled in Paris listed over 100 different crafts, each of which had its own association, or guild. By the 1420s, guilds existed in most big towns throughout Europe and their numbers were still growing. Their main objective was to gain high wages and exclusive control of their business for their members. They fixed prices and standards of work, and made sure that no outsiders competed with them. Guilds also supported members who fell on hard times, providing them with money from a central fund. In time, the guilds grew rich and powerful. They built grand guildhalls, paraded in fine dress on special occasions, and often played an important role in civic affairs.

THE ARMORERS
The Armorers' Guild maintained the standards of the craftsmen who made plate armor. Near Milan in Italy, one of the centers of armor-making in the 15th century, whole villages were employed in the trade.

Mail coif

Coiled wire

Rings snipped off wire

Rivets

Flap protects the mouth

Each ring end is flattened and linked by a rivet

ANOTHER FINE MESH
Mail-making was a skilled and painstaking process. Each ring was linked to four others and held together by a tiny rivet. An entire suit of mail could be made up of thousands of rings.

Pliers

WOMEN AT WORK
Most guilds would not allow women members, but this did not prevent women from learning skilled trades. Many worked with their husbands or fathers. Silk-weaving in London was almost entirely done by women, although they were not allowed to form their own guild.

Green comes from woad leaves and weld

Blue produced by woad or indigo dyes

Bright orange and red dyes come from madder roots

Linen dyed with madder root

Oak bark gives a brown color

Yellow comes from dyers' green weed, or weld

Plant-dyed wools

MASTER DYERS
In the Middle Ages, cloth-making was a gigantic industry that employed a large array of guild crafts. There were the weavers, the fullers and walkers (who cleaned and compacted the cloth), the carders (who brushed it), and the shearmen (who trimmed it). Then there were the dyers, who dyed the cloth in huge heated vats full of dyestuff (right).

The richer guilds had chambers in guildhalls, which proudly displayed their coats of arms. Here members met for a banquet on the anniversary of their patron saint, and the guild court sat to settle disputes and punish members who had disobeyed the strict rules.

"Borrelais" hat derived from a hood worn the wrong way around

Emblem of the Bakers' Guild

THE GUILD MASTER

This fine costume would have been worn by a middle-class merchant or business owner in the 1400s. Toward the end of the Middle Ages, the wealthier merchants began to control the guilds' affairs for their own ends. They bought the raw materials and sold the finished goods, and were more interested in making money than in the welfare of the poorer tradesmen. Guild masters also became important civic figures who often had the final say in the election of the town mayor.

Fashionable fur-trimmed sleeves

LEARNING A TRADE

Getting to the top of a guild was a long and hard process. An apprentice had to pay a large sum of money just to start. His apprenticeship lasted about seven years, during which time he learned every aspect of the craft from a master (seen here judging work by a mason and a carpenter). After this, he became a journeyman (from the French *journée*, or "day") and worked for a daily wage. A journeyman could one day become a master—as long as he paid the right fees.

Decorated leather purse

Personal eating knife

Blue woolen doublet lined with linen

Fine woolen coat made with a large amount of material as a sign of wealth

The codpiece, which served as a fly, became fashionable after 1450

Expensive midcalf leather boots

"Joined" hose were made to measure

Emblem of the Shoemakers' Guild

The stonemasons

OF ALL MEDIEVAL CRAFTSMEN, skilled masons were the most highly paid and respected. It was they who built the great cathedrals and castles that still rise above European towns and cities. Before they formed exclusive guilds (pp. 50–51) in the 14th century, masons organized their trade from their lodges. These were the masons' headquarters on the building site, where they worked under cover in bad weather, ate their meals, and discussed trade secrets. Rules and working conditions were set out by the lodge leaders. Masons learned their craft on the site itself, often serving an apprenticeship of up to seven years. The most talented might go on to become master masons, with the responsibility for designing and overseeing the building of an entire cathedral.

"Stock" rests on top of the stone

Blade measures depth

SINKING SQUARE
Each stone had to be worked precisely to shape before being hoisted into position. The sinking square was used to measure the depth of holes or grooves, and to check that the corners were square.

SCORING A CURVE
The mason had to mark out his stone to show him where to cut or carve. To mark a curved line parallel to the edge he used a box trammel. Holding the wooden handle firmly against the edge, he dragged it along. The trammel point moved across the stone, scoring a line.

Sharp point scores the stone

SQUARED UP
The square was one of the mason's most important tools. It was used for making sure corners were straight.

Well-worn chisel-head

Pitching tool for making clean breaks in rough stone

PITCHER THIS
Every single stone in a cathedral would have taken about a day to cut and finish. Because it was heavy and expensive to transport, the stone was cut approximately to size at the quarry. At the building site, the mason's first job was to finish cutting the rough stone with a big curved saw. Then he used a hammer, a heavy, blunt chisel called a pitching tool, and a punch (right) to chip off the larger lumps and produce nearly straight edges.

Hammer-headed chisels

Punch for chipping off large bits of stone

UNITED BY DIVIDERS
Dividers, or wing compasses, became the masons' special emblem. They were used mainly to measure a distance on a template, and then transfer the measurement to a piece of stone.

HEAVY LUMP
The lump hammer was used for hitting hammer-headed chisels in the rough shaping work. The softer the stone, the heavier the hammer.

Medieval dividers

Modern masons mark out a block with pencil lines

Paper template for a piece of window tracery

Template for the cross-section of the joint

Joint

ACCORDING TO PLAN
The pattern, or template, for each stone was cut out of board, leather, or parchment and laid over the stone for the mason to copy.

MARKING OUT
The mason selected a block of stone that had been trimmed square and smooth on which to mark out the template. He then scratched, or scribed, around the edges.

Drafting chisel for carving the first outline

Gouge for working curved surfaces

Claw chisel for scraping away stone

Mallet-headed chisels for use with a mallet

CHOOSING A CHISEL
An apprentice mason had to learn to handle a bewildering array of chisels. Each mason owned his own tools, all of which bore his personal mark. They were usually passed down from generation to generation. The design of modern masonry tools like those above has changed little since medieval times.

Stone relief dedicated to the Stonemasons' Guild, church of Orsanmichele, Florence, Italy

WORKS OF ART
Some stonemasons became specialized sculptors. Intricate carvings such as the figures, foliage, and animals that decorated the great cathedrals were created by highly skilled "imaginators."

MASTER MIND
The master mason was in charge of everything on the building site, from designing the building to hiring workers and ordering stone from the quarry. His job was that of an architect and a foreman all rolled into one—he set out plans and templates for his workers, but was also expected to work alongside them on occasion.

Cusp (from the Latin cuspis, *which means "spearhead")*

MASONS' MARK
A mason "signed" each finished stone with his personal mark to show how much work he had completed.

THE FINISHED ARTICLE
The carving of ornamental stonework—such as the stone ribs, or tracery, that supported stained glass windows—took many years to master. Experienced stonemasons could carve any number of complex pieces. This section of tracery links the delicate ribs in the upper part of a window.

SHAPING THE STONE
The final shaping of the stone was the job of a banker mason who worked on a bench, or banker. Using chisels, gouges, and saws, he cut the stone to the scribed pattern.

Masons rub away tool marks on soft stone with a toothed iron plate called a cock's comb, or drag

WORKING IN THE LODGE
Outside building work was only done in the good weather of the summer months. In winter, stonemasons labored on under cover in their lodge, designing, marking out, and cutting pieces of stone.

Fairs and feast days

BOTH PEASANTS AND TOWN-DWELLERS looked forward to the festivals and fairs that marked the important days of the year. On holy days, or holidays, such as Christmas and Easter, everyone took time off work to attend special church services, banquets, and festivities. Great trade fairs, often held on the feast days of saints, were also occasions for fun. Merchants came from all over Europe to buy and sell their goods, and they were entertained by musicians, acrobats, and players. Other special events that were related to different times of the year included May Day, Midsummer's Eve, and the Harvest Home.

NO DICE
Although it was frowned upon by the Church, gambling was one of the most widespread of medieval pastimes. People played dice games and betted on wrestling matches, cock fights, and bear baiting.

YULETIDE FOOLS
One of the highlights of Christmas was the Feast of Fools. A "bishop" was chosen and dressed up in mock vestments. He led everyone into church and recited services in gibberish. Meanwhile, others played dice on the altar and sang rude songs.

BALANCING ACT
Acrobats, jugglers, and dancing bears were all popular forms of entertainment at medieval festivals.

THE GREAT FAIRS
Fairs often grew out of religious festivals. After Nôtre-Dame Cathedral in Paris acquired a piece of Christ's "true cross" in 1109, thousands of pilgrims came to visit this holy relic (p. 42) each June. Merchants set up their stalls in the surrounding streets, and soon the fair had grown into a major event. The Bishop of Paris is seen here bestowing a blessing on the proceedings.

FAIR CHEWS
There was plenty of food on offer at fairs and markets. Simple baked or deep-fried meat pies like these "chewets" were the most common fare.

OUT ON THE TOWN
Many people came to fairs simply to have a good time, and tavern keepers did a roaring business. Large amounts of cheap ale and wine were consumed and drunkenness was common! In this Italian tavern, fresh quantities of wine are being passed up from the cellar to supply the carousing merchants.

Canvas
cover

New wooden
overshoes, or
pattens, for sale

Leather
flask, or
costrel

Leather
tankards

AT THE MARKET
Besides the great fairs,
there were weekly markets
in most big towns. Pedlars,
merchants, drovers of cattle,
sheep, pigs, and even geese,
all came. Stalls sold a huge
array of goods, from cheese,
eggs, and salt to pots and
pans, tools, knives, shoes,
and cloth. This reconstructed
medieval market stall
contains leather goods
that would have been
on sale at markets in the
14th and 15th centuries.

Colored
goatskin
for making
shoes

Large roll of
cattlehide for
shoe soles

Wooden frame can
be easily folded up
for transporting
the stall

Wooden shoe
"lasts" for
shoemaking

Old shoes waiting
to be mended

Leftover leather from
cutout shoe patterns

Leather
bottles

Medieval music

In the middle ages, most people heard music in church. In the echoing spaces of the great cathedrals, monks and priests recited their texts by chanting them in a single key. This lovely form of singing was known as plainchant or plainsong. Few cathedrals had organs, and church singing was usually unaccompanied by musical instruments, but kings and noblemen often dined to the sound of harps and lutes played by poet-musicians called troubadours (p. 26). On feast days, ordinary people sang folksongs and danced to pipes and drums and, by 1400, most towns had a town band of professional musicians who accompanied processions with shawms (p. 58) and trumpets.

BEAR FOOT
Some musicians trained bears to dance and tumble to the music of the pipe and tabor. Bears were used because they could walk on two feet in a human way.

A MEDIEVAL DRUM KIT
Many musical instruments were brought to Europe by returning crusaders. These small drums, or nakers (left), were modeled on the Middle-Eastern *naqqara*, a kind of kettledrum with a curved body. Nakers were hung in pairs on a belt and usually played to accompany dance music.

Nakers player

Hurdy-gurdy player

Turning the handle operates the instrument

The turning wheel plays the strings

FINE FIDDLE
Most troubadours in 13th-century France accompanied themselves on a fiddle. It was bigger than the modern violin and often rested in the lap. This fiddle had one string that could be altered on the fingerboard. The other four were fixed strings that sounded a continuous bass note, or drone.

SYMPHONY OF SOUND
Monks in 11th-century Spain used an organistrum to teach singing in their choir schools. This was a stringed instrument that needed two people to operate. One turned the handle while the other played the keys. The organistrum developed into the hurdy-gurdy, which could be played by one man. It could mingle several sounds together, so came to be known as the "symphony."

Wheel-cover

Drumstick

ONE MAN BAND
The smallest of all dance bands was the pipe and tabor. The pipe had only three holes, and the musician could easily play it with his left hand, while hitting the tabor with his right. These simple instruments were commonly used to accompany village dances.

Pipe

Bagpipes player

Sound comes out through pipes

The strings are plucked with goose quills

"nare"
lds a buzz
the sound
the tabor

HEAVENLY MUSIC
In medieval paintings, angels were often shown playing the psaltery. Similar to a small harp, it often formed part of a small orchestra, played with other soft instruments such as the lute (p. 44), the viol, or the flute.

Musician blows into mouthpiece to inflate the bag

Pipe is played with fingers

Pegs can be tightened to tune the strings

Keys operate the two inside strings

Keys fall back into place by gravity

Outside strings are bass strings, or drones

BAGPIPES
Contrary to legend, bagpipes were not invented by the Scots. In fact, in about 1300 they were being played in many parts of the world, including England, India, and North Africa.

Bag is made of leather

Plays and parades

Medieval drama was started by the Church. Sometime in the 11th century, priests began to add short scenes to the major religious services, such as those at Christmas and Easter. The scenes portrayed the great moments in the Bible—the fall of Adam, Noah escaping the flood, or Samson destroying the temple. People loved this new kind of entertainment. The scenes became so popular that they were performed in church porches, then on stages in town market places where more people could see them. By the 13th century, they had become complete cycles of plays, telling the whole Christian story and lasting as long as 40 days. In England, France, Italy, and Germany, they were staged by the local guilds (p. 50). They became known as "mystery" plays, from the French word *métier*, or trade.

MASKS AND MUMMERS
Horses' heads, devil masks, drums, bells, and dances all played their part in a performance put on by mummers (above). On special occasions, mummers, or masked actors, staged short plays or mimes that told simple folk tales, usually featuring dramatic sword fights and a doctor, who would enter at the end of the story and bring the dead back to life.

WILD GREEN MEN
Many pagan (non-Christian) rituals lived on in medieval Europe. Bands of "wodwos," or wild woodsmen, dressed in leaves and greenery would rush into feasts and pageants, wreaking havoc. Their dances symbolized the untamed forces of Nature. On the occasion shown above, their costumes accidentally caught on fire from a candle!

The dragon can be made to "breathe" fire and smoke from its mouth by exploding small amounts of gunpowder inside its head

FUNNY FACE
In 1230, a priest complained of actors who "change and distort their bodies with shameful leaps and gestures." This stone carving shows a fool or jester literally "pulling a face" to amuse his audience. Fools also entertained people by telling crude jokes and waving a pig's bladder filled with dried peas.

FESTIVAL FANFARE
The shawm was a reed instrument with a loud, piercing sound that was played at town parades and festivals.

PLAYING THE DEVIL

Like church carvings and stained glass windows (pp. 34–35), mystery plays were a way of teaching the Bible stories to ordinary people who could not read and write. In this scene, the Devil is seen tempting Jesus in the wilderness. Each section of a mystery play was mounted on a wagon and drawn to a series of stations throughout the town. If spectators waited long enough in one spot, they would see the whole cycle of plays.

Carved wooden head decorated with bright paint

SNAP DRAGON

This wooden head belonged to a parade dragon that was used in processions to celebrate the feast day of St. George in the town of Norwich, England. It was operated by a man hidden inside the basketwork body, and it caused great amusement by snapping at the people who lined the streets. Dragons also played an important part in many mummers' plays, in which they were usually shown battling against the valiant St. George.

The back of the dragon's head was fitted with a long wooden pole, which was used for maneuvering the head

Lower jaw can be pulled up to make a snapping noise

Death and disease

DEATH WAS EVER-PRESENT for people living in the Middle Ages. Medical knowledge was limited and the average life expectancy was about 30 years. Frequent wars and famines claimed thousands of lives at a time, and disease was rife in the dirty, overcrowded streets of medieval towns and cities. The most catastrophic event of all was the Black Death. Carried by black rats, it was brought back from Asia by Italian sailors. The plague was deadly and highly contagious. Symptoms included black and blue blotches on the body, and no cure was ever found. It swept through Europe between 1347 and 1350. By the end of 1348, at least a third of the entire population of Europe had died.

FEVERFEW
Strong-smelling feverfew was used to treat headaches and to assist in childbirth.

MARJORAM
Marjoram was used to make healing poultices to place on bruises and swellings.

LEMON BALM
This plant was seen as a kind of magic elixir that could cure serious illnesses. It was also used for fevers and colds because it causes sweating.

LUNGWORT
Because the shape of its leaves resembled lungs, lungwort was used to treat chest disorders.

HERBAL MEDICINE
Medieval medicine was based mainly on folklore and superstition rather than scientific observation. For example, many medical handbooks recommended that healing herbs should be picked on magical days of the year, such as Midsummer's Eve. However, many of the herbs in use in medieval times are still employed by herbalists today.

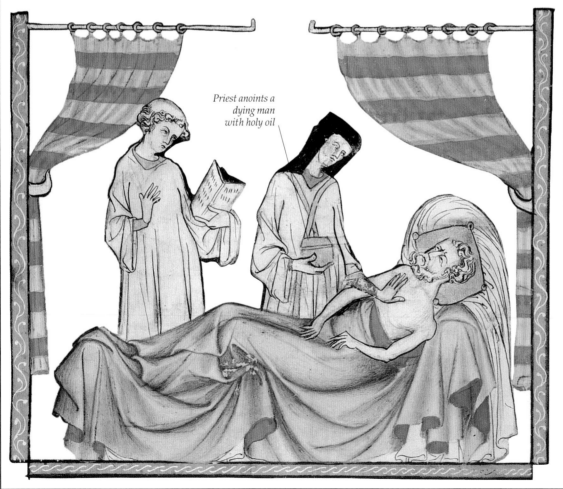

Priest anoints a dying man with holy oil

PERFORMING SURGERY
The most common form of surgery was bloodletting (above), which was performed by uneducated barber-surgeons. People believed it restored the balance of the body's fluids, but more often it seriously weakened already sick patients.

LAST RITES
People in the Middle Ages believed it was important to die properly. If they did not make a final confession of their sins to a priest, they thought that they would go to hell (p. 31). But as the Black Death raged, so many priests perished that most of the people who died were buried without prayers or ceremony.

Preparations were often stored in sheep's horns

Linen bung for powder container

Tooth powder was fairly abrasive

WORMWOOD
Wormwood was used to rid the digestive system of worms and was also placed in clothes to repel fleas.

Whelk shell

AT THE DENTIST
Without modern painkillers, most medieval surgical treatments must have been fairly unpleasant. Rotten teeth were yanked out by tooth-pullers who worked at weekly markets.

Oyster shell

Cuttlefish bone

MEDIEVAL TOOTHPASTE
Ingredients like these were ground up to make powder for cleaning teeth. Such preparations would have been used by wealthy people mainly for cosmetic purposes, since there was no knowledge of the need for dental hygiene. Breath was sweetened with honey and coriander or cumin seeds.

PLAGUE PITS
At the height of the Black Death, people had to carry their own dead to mass burial pits because there were not enough coffins to go around. In Paris, France, nearly 800 people died every day. Simple lead crosses such as these were placed on the corpses.

Skeleton dances to a pipe and tabor (p. 57)

THE DANCE OF DEATH
The theme of death as the great leveler was acted out in the macabre Dance of Death. Men dressed as skeletons danced with figures representing each level of society to show that death comes to all. The Dance of Death was also depicted in many church carvings, paintings, and manuscripts.

Fearful monk is dragged off by the deathly dancer

FEAR OF THE PLAGUE
"This is the end of the World!" lamented an Italian chronicler of the Black Death. Many believed the plague was divine punishment for human sins, and the Church held special services and processions.

The birth of a new age

RELIGIOUS REFORMER
The religious Reformation was spearheaded by a German priest named Martin Luther (1483–1546). In 1517, he wrote a list of 95 arguments against Roman Catholic practices and nailed them to the door of Wittenberg Cathedral, provoking a wave of protest against the Church.

IN THE 15TH CENTURY, there was a rebirth, or "renaissance," of interest in the arts and sciences. During the Renaissance, which began in Italy, works of the great Latin and Greek writers were rediscovered and studied for the first time since the fall of Rome. They inspired artists and scholars to turn away from a strictly religious view of life and concentrate on human beings. Renaissance painters and sculptors began to explore the beauty of the human body, and poets wrote about human feelings and experiences. These new ideas also caused people to question traditional views on religion. Many thought that the Catholic Church (pp. 30–31) had become corrupt and needed change. A group of reformers called the Protestants rejected the authority of the Pope in Rome and set up new churches in northern Europe. This movement became known as the Reformation. It divided the Christian world and brought to an end the all-encompassing power of the medieval Church.

Handpainted decoration

Gothic type imitates handwritten text

THE PRINTED WORD
Few inventions have changed the world as dramatically as printing with metal type. Printing was developed in Europe by Johannes Gutenberg (c. 1398–1468), who produced the first printed Bible in the 1450s. This process replaced copying laboriously by hand, which made books rare and expensive.

PATRON OF PAINTERS
The Italian city of Florence was at the center of the artistic Renaissance. This was due largely to men such as Lorenzo de' Medici (1449–1492). Nicknamed "the Magnificent," he used his wealth to employ artists such as Michelangelo (p. 7).

NEW SCHOOLS
Before the Renaissance, nearly all schools were run by the Church. Afterward, many new grammar schools were founded by rich merchants and noblemen. The spread of education was hastened by the wider availability of books.

CONSTANTINOPLE FALLS
The Middle Ages ended as they began, with the invaders from the East. This time it was the Ottoman Turks. In 1453, after a long siege, they conquered Constantinople, which became the Muslim city of Istanbul. It was the end of the thousand-year-old Christian Byzantine Empire in the East (p. 6).

RENAISSANCE MAN
Leonardo da Vinci (1452–1519) embodied the spirit of the Renaissance. He was a brilliant painter and sculptor who also had an avid interest in science, engineering, and architecture. His most famous painting is the *Mona Lisa*, but he also produced detailed anatomical drawings, and sketches for numerous inventions, such as this flying machine.

NEW FIREPOWER
The development of guns made an enormous difference to warfare after the mid-14th century. Cannons could break down stone walls, bringing an end to the era of the impenetrable castle.

THE GREAT NAVIGATORS
In the 15th century, Europeans embarked on great voyages of discovery as they searched for sea routes to Asia. From the 1420s, Portuguese sailors ventured down the long west coast of Africa in caravels like this one. In 1488, Bartholomew Diaz rounded the Cape of Good Hope and sailed into the Indian Ocean for the first time. By 1498, Vasco da Gama had reached India. Meanwhile, Christopher Columbus crossed the Atlantic in 1492 and claimed America for the Spanish king.

Did you know?

Since clean water was difficult to come by in the Middle Ages, ale or wine was drunk with most meals. Peasants made wine by harvesting ripe grapes, crushing them underfoot, then fermenting the juice.

Although wealthy people imported carpets from the East during the Middle Ages, the carpets were too precious to be laid on the floor. Instead, they were draped over tables.

The walls of grand houses were hung with tapestries, heavy fabrics, and leather panels, which added color to the rooms, provided insulation against the cold, and displayed the family's wealth.

Textiles were an important part of a rich man's bed: beds of the wealthy consisted of a rudimentary wooden frame hung with opulent drapes that were intended as much to reflect status as to afford privacy and warmth.

Seating in early medieval homes consisted mainly of benches built along the walls. At a time when violence was widespread, people had to make sure nobody could sneak up behind them.

Blacksmiths played a central role in medieval society, since they manufactured and mended every object made of metal, from chains, nails, tools, pots, locks, hinges, and handles to weapons, wagon fittings, and horseshoes.

Peasants were required to spend at least one day a week doing laboring jobs for their lord. They carried stones for his new buildings, mended bridges and roads, and cut down trees for his firewood.

Medieval men and women usually slept naked, even in winter; one documented marriage contract from the 13th century even forbade a wife from wearing nightclothes without her husband's consent.

Autumn, 1531, a painting of a town market by the German medieval artist Jörg Breu the Elder

Late medieval beds were warmed with long-handled brass pans filled with burning embers from the fire. Occasionally, these pans were also used for smuggling healthy babies into noble ladies' chambers to replace still-born heirs.

Rich people in the Middle Ages wore sumptuous—frequently woolen—clothes; individual garments were sometimes stored in smelly toilets, however, to discourage moths.

Horseshoe

In larger houses, animals were often stabled on the ground floor so their body heat would rise up through the wooden floorboards and help to warm the main rooms.

Another common source of heat was the brazier, a freestanding basket or pot—sometimes on a stand—in which charcoal or coal was burned. Convenient and portable, braziers could also be dangerous, since burning charcoal gives off carbon monoxide gas.

Early fireplaces were commonly adorned with images inspired by nature. The one in Queen Eleanor's 13th-century chamber at Westminster displayed a figure of Winter with a "sad countenance" and "miserable contortions of the body."

The right to hold a weekly market could only be granted to a town by the king in a document called a charter. Since markets brought trade and prosperity to a growing community, such a charter was of vital importance.

Infants' cradles were frequently made from birch wood, which was believed to repel evil spirits. (Elder, in contrast, was thought to attract them.)

Slender, shapely legs were considered very masculine in medieval times: to show them off, fashionable men wore short or close-fitting pants with woolen hose.

Tight boots accentuated calves

Henry VII coin

Q Was the structure of a royal court during the medieval era as formal and complex as popular mythology suggests?

A In our less regimented age, it's difficult to imagine the rigid and intricate hierarchy that surrounded medieval kings and queens. The bed of Henry VII of England, for example, required a retinue of attendants just to maintain it: there was a gentleman usher to draw the curtains; a groom to carry in fresh straw regularly for the mattress; a squire and yeoman to tie, lay, and test it for concealed weapons, then cover it with canvas, a feather bed (like a comforter), and perfumed sheets and blankets; and a special squire of the body to anoint the bed with holy water. Any necessary textile repairs were made by designated sewers, curtains were changed by more lowly staff called yeoman hangers, and running maintenance was undertaken by similarly humble, but often quite specialized, personnel.

Q How did the criminal justice system work during the Middle Ages?

A The local lord would settle disputes within his own manor and decide on the most suitable punishment for each crime. Some offenders would be executed, others would be fined, and those who had committed minor misdemeanours were likely to be sentenced to a period in the stocks or pillories: wooden contraptions equipped with holes in which a captive's ankles (stocks) or wrists and head (pillories) would be locked. These devices were set up in public places, and as part of the punishment, passers-by were encouraged to throw rotten fruit. On the whole, only military and political prisoners were shut away, usually within a large castle.

Q How safe were the streets of a medieval town?

A During the day, with the bustle of the crowds and markets, the most common dangers came from pickpockets and dishonest traders. When the Sun went down, though, the pitch-dark streets harbored robbers and violent criminals. At dusk, therefore, bells were rung to sound the curfew—the time when, by law, everyone had to be indoors. After this time, nightwatchmen patrolled the streets with candle lanterns to discourage villains and catch anyone who was out after curfew.

French book illustration from about 1206, showing townspeople taunting a woman in the pillories

Record breakers

Westminster Abbey, London, England

UNBROKEN LINK
With the exception of Edward V and Edward VIII (who were never crowned), every English monarch since 1066 has been crowned in Westminster Abbey, London. The original building was consecrated in 1065, but it was later demolished. The Abbey was largely rebuilt by 1272, and finally completed during the 18th century.

LONDON BRIDGE IS GOING UP
The first stone bridge across the Thames River in London was commissioned by Henry II in 1170. It was completed in 1206, after Henry's death. With its drawbridge, double row of houses, and 140 shops, it became one of the world's most famous bridges, and it remained the only stone Thames bridge until 1750.

DEADLY ENEMY
The biggest killer ever to hit Europe, the Black Death (bubonic plague) wiped out 25 million people—one-third of the total population—in the three years between 1347 and 1350.

POTENT SYMBOL
One of the most durable product symbols in history has its origins in medieval times. Beers and ales of the day, just like their modern equivalents, varied widely in strength, so their containers were labeled accordingly: "X" for the weakest, up to "XXXX" for the most potent. In 1924, an Australian brewery revived the "XXXX" symbol, which is still widely advertised and recognized today.

Who's who?

Richard the Lionheart

THE FEUDAL TERRITORIES OF MEDIEVAL EUROPE were totally dominated by those who held land, power, and money: the kings, emperors, and nobles. A smaller group of people—rebels and revolutionaries—dedicated their lives to changing the status quo. Observing and recording the times they lived in, artists, writers, and scientists produced work that helped to spread knowledge, enrich spirits, and enhance our modern historical understanding.

POWER AND NOBILITY

Charlemagne

CHARLEMAGNE (742–814)
King of the Franks (early inhabitants of France), Charlemagne united much of modern France and Germany. A great leader, lawmaker, and champion of arts and literature, he was also a legendary warrior. Charlemagne was crowned the first Holy Roman Emperor by Pope Leo III.

ALFRED THE GREAT (c. 846–899)
Initially King of Wessex, Alfred made peace with the Viking leader Guthrum under the Treaty of Wedmore and assumed control of all England. As ruler, he reformed Saxon law, promoted education, and commissioned the *Anglo-Saxon Chronicle*, a history of the English people.

KING CNUT (CANUTE) (c. 994–1035)
When the Viking Svein Forkbeard died in 1014, his son Cnut inherited his Danish crown but was challenged to his father's English throne. After two years of conflict, however, Cnut triumphed, becoming the respected king of an empire that was soon to include Norway and southern Sweden as well as Denmark and England.

WILLIAM THE CONQUEROR (c. 1027–1087)
Aggrieved that the English throne went to Harold, Earl of Wessex, when it had been pledged to him by Edward the Confessor, William of Normandy invaded England in 1066 and defeated Harold at the Battle of Hastings. As king, he brought stability and introduced the feudal system.

FREDERICK I (BARBAROSSA) (c. 1121–1190)
Holy Roman Emperor from 1152, Frederick I (his nickname means "Red Beard") unified the German states. He drowned crossing a river on his way to the 3rd Crusade.

HENRY II (1133–1189)
Only 21 when he became English king, Henry Plantagenet was involved in reforming the Church. Lord of an empire that also included much of France, Henry also laid the foundation for common law, including the right to trial by jury (*see also* St. Thomas Becket).

SALADIN (c. 1137–1193)
Chivalrous sultan of Egypt who led Muslim resistance to the Crusader armies. He recaptured Jerusalem and parts of Palestine from them.

RICHARD I (1157–1199)
Known as "the Lionheart," King Richard ruled England for 10 years, most of which he spent at war in France and on the 3rd Crusade. One of England's most celebrated kings, he passed just seven months of his reign at home.

PHILIP II (1165–1223)
Ruler of France from 1180, Philip, also known as Philip Augustus, fought three English kings—Henry II, Richard I, and John—to gain control of their French territories, a goal he finally accomplished in 1214.

KING JOHN (1167–1216)
Younger brother of Richard I, John is remembered mainly as the signatory of Magna Carta (Great Charter): its limiting of royal power was a milestone in English constitutional history.

FREDERICK II (1194–1250)
Holy Roman Emperor from 1220, Frederick led the Sixth Crusade, returning Jerusalem temporarily to Christian rule. A religious sceptic, he was considered the most cultured man of his time.

LOUIS IX (1214–1270)
Outstandingly moral and brave king of France, Louis was revered across Europe and fought in two Crusades. He died of the plague on his way to lead the 8th Crusade, and he was later canonized (made a saint).

PHILIP VI (1293–1350)
Philip was the first French king of the house of Valois, which was based in the province of Burgundy. Inherited in 1328, his crown was challenged by Edward III of England, who defeated him in battle at Crécy in 1346. Edward later surrendered his claim in return for French territories.

EDWARD III (1312–1377)
English ruler and instigator (in 1337) of the Hundred Years' War in support of his claim to the French throne. Edward was also responsible for major legal and parliamentary reform at home. His son, also called Edward, was a great soldier known as the Black Prince because of the color of his armor.

Edward the Confessor

HENRY V (c. 1387–1422)
Inheriting the English throne in 1413, Henry redoubled the war against France and defeated the French at Agincourt in 1415. By 1420, he had established himself as the French heir, but he died before he could succeed, and all his conquests were lost in the reign of his son Henry VI (*see also* Joan of Arc).

VLAD TEPES (c. 1430–1476)
Romanian baron who murdered thousands of people by impaling them on stakes, earning him the nickname "Vlad the Impaler." His unparalleled cruelty provided the basis of the Dracula legend.

REBELLION AND REFORMATION

St. Francis of Assisi

ST. FRANCIS OF ASSISI (C. 1182–1226)
A rich man who gave his fortune away, Francis founded the Franciscan order of friars, who traveled around preaching, begging for food, and communing with nature and animals.

SIMON DE MONTFORT (C. 1208–1265)
Organizer of a group of English barons who challenged King Henry III to reform his government—a council the king could consult at will. Defeating Henry in 1264, de Montfort summoned the first English Parliament, which included knights from each shire and citizens from the major cities and towns.

WAT TYLER (D. 1381)
Leader of the English peasant revolt of 1381. King Richard II initially agreed to their demands to abolish high rents, serfdom, and the poll tax, but he later recanted. During the fighting, Wat Tyler was killed by the Mayor of London.

JOAN OF ARC (C. 1412–1431)
Peasant girl who led the French armies against the English forces of Henry VI. She was captured by the enemy and burned at the stake in Rouen, France, in 1431.

SAVONAROLA (1452–1498)
Italian friar, orator, and reformer who led a revolt in Florence, Italy, that expelled the powerful Medici family and then established a republic. He also denounced the corrupt pope, Alexander VI, who had him tortured and burned for heresy.

Joan of Arc (from a book illustration)

ST. BENEDICT (C. 480–C. 550)
Founder of the Benedictine religious order and creator of its vows of poverty, chastity, and obedience. Known as "St. Benedict's Rule," these vows were eventually adopted by holy orders across Europe.

ST. THOMAS BECKET (1118–1170)
Henry II's Archbishop of Canterbury and close friend, Becket quarreled with the king about Church reform. As a result, four of Henry's knights murdered him, and he was later canonized.

ARTS AND SCIENCES

ST. BEDE (VENERABLE BEDE) (C. 673–735)
English monk and scholar who wrote, among other important works, the *Ecclesiastical History of the English Nation*, a primary source for students of English history. He also produced a history of the saints, a study of holy martyrs, and a textbook to help his pupils write poetry in Latin.

AVICENNA (C. 980–1037)
Arabian philosopher and physician whose *Canon Medicinae (Canon of Medicine)* combined his own knowledge with that of Roman and Arabic physicians. It became the standard medical work for centuries.

GIOTTO (C. 1267–1337)
Born in Florence, Italy, Giotto di Bondone founded the central tradition of Western painting. He had an enormous influence on Renaissance artists such as Masaccio and Michelangelo.

Geoffrey Chaucer

GEOFFREY CHAUCER (C. 1340–1400)
One of the greatest poets of the Middle Ages, Chaucer is best known for his *Canterbury Tales*, a collection of stories told by pilgrims on their way to Thomas Becket's shrine in Canterbury.

CHRISTINE DE PISAN (C. 1364–1429)
One of the few medieval women to write books and poetry professionally (at this time, few women could read and write), Christine de Pisan often dealt with feminist issues.

JOHANNES GUTENBERG (C. 1398–1468)
German inventor of printing using movable metal type arranged in words and lines, instead of the solid printing blocks for each page that were used previously. Gutenberg printed two early versions of the Bible.

JAN VAN EYCK (D. 1441)
Born in Flanders (present-day Belgium), Jan van Eyck is one of the most revered of all early painters. Although much of his youthful history is uncertain, his mastery of color and detail left an unequaled model for his successors throughout the Renaissance and beyond. His paintings provide a unique insight into the quality of medieval life.

Johannes Gutenberg (far right) in his workshop

Find out more

BECAUSE MOST EXISTING MEDIEVAL BUILDINGS are imposing monuments, such as castles or cathedrals, rather than domestic dwellings, they don't give us much idea about what everyday life was like when they were built. Also, because the Middle Ages are so far removed—and so different—from our own time, it takes a lot more learning and imagination to create a mental picture of this time than it does to imagine the more recent past.

Ways you can find out more about the medieval world include looking at websites and other illustrated books and, if possible, visiting museums or visitor attractions that attempt to conjure up the atmosphere of life hundreds of years ago. One such attraction is Bede's World in northeastern England. It focuses on the life and times of the Venerable Bede, a monk who lived 1,300 years ago (p. 67). The complex includes a museum and a recreated medieval village with an experimental farm that has three large buildings constructed in the way they would have been in St. Bede's day.

HE WELCOMES A YOUNG MAN CALLED BEDE TO THE MONASTERY.

VENERABLE BEDE
In this medieval-style icon created in the 21st century by Peter Murphy, Bede is welcomed to the monastery at Jarrow in northeast England by his patron Benedict Biscop (pronounced Bishop). Biscop was a local nobleman and intellectual whose travels to Rome inspired him to create the enlightened atmosphere in which Bede flourished.

Modern Northumberland cross in 8th-century style

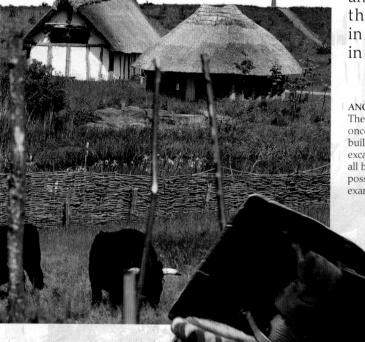

ANCIENT FARM
The demonstration farm at Bede's World was once a derelict fuel-storage site. Its reconstructed buildings are based on medieval examples excavated locally, while the crops and animals are all bred to resemble primitive stock as closely as possible: the dexter cattle in the foreground, for example, are smaller than most modern breeds.

Heraldic colors repeated on shield

Some surcoats had short sleeves

MODERN TOURNAMENTS
In many countries, medieval societies stage authentic reenactments of large-scale battles or tournaments. In this mock 15th-century skirmish at Goodrich Castle in England, two knights in full body armor wear distinctive surcoats that bear the heraldic motif of their respective lords.

ABBEY OF MONT-ST-MICHEL, FRANCE
The Benedictine monks who still live in this medieval abbey take all their meals in this lofty, sunlit refectory near the building's highest level . The simple life they lead here carries on traditions that were first established by St. Benedict during the 10th century.

Censer suspended from gilt chains

ANCIENT RITUALS
In some Christian churches, censers, or incense burners, are swung from side to side to disperse a rich, smoky fragrance during services. In medieval times, rituals involving incense were an important part of worship in the Catholic Church, which dominated society.

Helmet trimmed with gold

BURIAL TREASURE
Discovered in a burial mound excavated at Sutton Hoo, Suffolk, England, in 1939, this spectacular iron helmet is thought to have belonged to a local ruler during the 7th century. The helmet, along with other objects from Sutton Hoo, is on display at the British Museum.

Places to visit

METROPOLITAN MUSEUM OF ART, NEW YORK, NY
Although "the Met" displays some of its rich medieval collection in the main building on Fifth Avenue, most of it is at The Cloisters in north Manhattan. The museum's only branch, it was constructed during the 1930s from fragments of medieval architecture brought back from Europe. Worth seeing are:
• the life-sized tomb effigy of a 13th-century crusader
• the apse from a 12th-century Spanish church, which contains 3,000 limestone blocks
• the deck of 15th-century playing cards adorned with hunting images and symbols

CLEVELAND MUSEUM OF ART, CLEVELAND, OH
The Cleveland Museum of Art is internationally renowned for its extensive medieval holdings, which include many acknowledged masterpieces:
• the Guelph Treasure, a dazzling group of gilded, jewel-encrusted religious objects, held for centuries by the German nobility
• three alabaster mourners from the tomb of Philip the Bold, Duke of Burgurdy
• an exquisite 14th-century table fountain

THE WALTERS ART MUSEUM, BALTIMORE, MD
Baltimore's premier art museum features an impressive gallery of medieval art. Highlights of the collection include:
• the silver reliquary of Saint Pantaleon, made in the shape of an arm
• a beautiful copper-and-enamel crozier depicting the annunciation
• an impressive array of carved ivory boxes and book covers

THE GETTY CENTER, LOS ANGELES, CA
Known for its architecture and spectacular views, the Getty also has plenty of interest for budding medievalists:
• a world-renowned collection of illustrated manuscripts, dating from the 9th to the 16th centuries
• a Sacred Art gallery, featuring stained-glass panels and other religious objects from the Middle Ages and early Renaissance

MEDIEVAL TIMES DINNER & TOURNAMENT, VARIOUS LOCATIONS
This chain of entertainment venues gives you the chance to watch a live medieval jousting tournament as you eat your meal. Although the shows contain more than a touch of Hollywood fantasy and special effects, the franchise is committed to the historical accuracy of the jousters' costumes and weapons.

12th-century casket adorned with scenes of Thomas Becket's murder

Glossary

ARTISAN Skilled craftsman such as a metalworker, carpenter, or stone mason.

BARON Highest-ranking noble; barons received their fief directly from the monarch (*see also* FIEF).

BISHOP Powerful church official, equal in status to a baron. Each bishop ruled over a large administrative area called a diocese, controlling all the priests and monasteries within it.

BUTTERY Room where food and drink are prepared and stored.

BUTTRESS Stone or brick mass built against the external walls of a large building, such as a cathedral, to give additional strength. Buttresses are usually positioned at points of stress caused by roofs, arches, or vaults.

CHAMLET Early cloth woven from wool and goat's hair that was widely used for everyday garments.

CORDWAINER Medieval term for shoemaker, from the city of Cordoba in Spain, which was associated with fine shoe leather.

COSTREL Small leather flask traditionally used by peasant farmers for carrying ale into the fields.

COURTIER One of the officials and nobles who served the monarch at court.

DAIS Raised platform at one end of a great hall, where the lord's table was positioned.

DAUB A mixture of clay, straw, and dung plastered over wattle for insulation, forming a wattle-and-daub wall (*see also* WATTLE).

DEMESNE The land belonging directly to a lord, as opposed to his manor—the land controlled by him (*see also* MANOR).

FALCONRY Practice of keeping and training falcons; in medieval times, falcons were mainly used for hunting.

Falconry

Lancet windows, Timoleague Abbey, Ireland

FALLOW Description of farm land left uncultivated so it can regain the nutrients used up by repeated planting.

FAST Period of abstinence from all or some types of food as a religious observance.

FENESTRAL WINDOW Type of window with a wooden frame. Over this was stretched resin-and-tallow-soaked linen, which let in light and reduced drafts.

FEUDAL SYSTEM System of land and power distribution based on the allocation of land in return for services.

FIEF Land that was held under the feudal system (*see also* FEUDAL SYSTEM).

FREEHOLDER Person who owned his own land, as opposed to being allowed the use of it under the feudal system (*see also* FEUDAL SYSTEM).

GARGOYLE Water spout carved in the form of a grotesque human or animal figure that projects from a roof, wall, or tower.

GLEBE Village land belonging to a parish priest, where he grew his own food.

GUILD Company or association connected with a particular craft or skill, such as shoemaking, weaving, or masonry. Many of the guilds established during the Middle Ages still exist today.

HABIT Distinctive robes worn by monks and nuns to indicate their vocation, and often their order.

HALL Principal and largest domestic space in a medieval palace or home, where family, officials, and servants spent most of their time.

HERETIC Someone who expressed an opinion that contradicted church doctrine.

HIPPOCRAS Medieval drink made from wine mixed with honey and herbs.

Knight on horseback

JOUST Competition between two knights in which they rode toward each other, each trying to knock the other off his horse.

KNIGHT Nobly born and armored warrior on horseback. Some knights served a lord, others were lords themselves.

LANCET WINDOW Tall, slender window with a pointed arch at the top, very popular in the 13th century.

LEWIS Iron tool used for gripping heavy blocks of stone so they can be lifted.

LORD Male knight or noble, often holder of a castle and estate that provided a living for his family, his servants, and the peasants on his land.

Gargoyle

MANOR Territory under the control of a lord: usually his house or castle, a village, a church, and the surrounding land.

MANOR HOUSE The home of a lord and lady and the center of community life. Manor houses, even if they weren't castles, were usually well fortified against attack.

MINSTREL Wandering performer during the Middle Ages who wrote and sang songs, played an instrument, and wrote poetry.

MOOR Member of the Muslim ruling class in Spain during the Middle Ages.

MUMMER Actor, usually one of a traveling troupe that put on plays.

NOBLE Person belonging to the aristocracy by birth or rank, such as a baron, knight, or bishop (*see also* BARON, KNIGHT).

PEASANTS People who worked on a lord's estate in return for a small plot of land on which they could grow crops to feed themselves and their families.

PEDDLER Salesman who traveled from place to place hawking an assortment of small, inexpensive items.

PEWTER Metal alloy (usually containing tin, lead, and copper) widely used during the Middle Ages for objects such as tableware, candlesticks, and jewelry.

PILGRIM Someone who traveled to a sacred place as an act of religious devotion; such journeys were called pilgrimages.

PLAINSONG Also called plainchant, a style of unaccompanied chanting used by medieval monks to recite their sacred texts. Plainsong has a single melodic line that follows the rhythm of the words.

POTTAGE Thick soup or stew made from vegetables, grain, and meat stock.

SCUTAGE Specific payment (also called shield money) payable by a vassal to his lord in lieu of military service.

SEEDLIP Small basket for seeds being sown by hand.

SERF Peasant laborer, also called a villein. Serfs virtually belonged to their lord, who allowed them a small piece of land on which to live and work in exchange for labor under the feudal system (*see also* FEUDAL SYSTEM).

SHAWM Early reed instrument with a piercing sound (forerunner of the oboe) that was popular for parades and festivals.

SICKLE Handled implement with a curved blade used for harvesting crops or trimming growth.

SMITH Metal worker. A blacksmith works in iron, a goldsmith in gold.

SOLAR Private room for a noble and his family, away from the largely communal spaces that dominated most castles and manor houses.

STOCKS Instrument of public punishment consisting of a wooden frame with holes for the prisoner's ankles. Passers-by were encouraged to jeer and throw rotten fruit. Pillories held a prisoner's neck and wrists in the same way.

STYLUS Writing implement used by medieval scholars to scratch letters onto wax tablets.

SURCOAT Tunic worn over a knight's armor, bearing the heraldic motif of his lord.

TITHE Ten percent portion of everything a peasant produced that had to be given to the local priest.

TONSURE Style of shaving a monk's or priest's head, usually on the crown, to indicate his status.

TOURNAMENT Popular entertainment featuring mock skirmishes. In addition to giving pleasure to the crowd, tournaments provided practice for real warfare.

TOURNEY Mock battle staged as part of a tournament (see also TOURNAMENT).

TRENCHER Thick slab of stale bread used as a plate. Having soaked up any gravy or juices, trenchers were either eaten by the diners themselves, given to the poor, or fed to the animals.

TRENTAL Package of 30 masses (services) said on behalf of an individual or family in exchange for a large payment to the church.

TROUBADOUR Medieval poet/musician, especially one who specialized in ballads of courtly love.

TRUCKLE BED Small bed that rolls out on wheels from under a larger one, used in medieval times to accommodate a child or servant. Also called a trundle bed.

VASSAL Someone who owes services to another person in return for land under the feudal system (*see also* FEUDAL SYSTEM).

VILLEIN see SERF

Wattle-and-daub construction

VISOR Flap on the front of a helmet that can be pulled down to protect the face.

WASTEL Type of fine white bread eaten only by the rich. Poor people ate coarse whole-wheat loaves.

WATTLE Interwoven branches used to form the basic structure of walls (*see also* DAUB).

WIMPLE Headdress worn by medieval women (and still by some nuns). Wimples wound around the head, down over the ears and under the chin, falling in folds across the neck for maximum coverage.

WINDLASS Machine for hauling or lifting heavy objects (such as building blocks) using a wheel and axle.

WRIT Signed document, usually from a monarch or a high-ranking official, passing a law or granting permission for something.

Distinctive shaved head or tonsure

Medieval monk

Shawm

A wimple is fastened to the hair with pins

Wimple

Index

ABC

Acknowledgments

The Publisher would like to thank:
The York Archaeological Trust for Excavation and Research Ltd.; Richard Fitch and Mark Meltonville of Wolfbane; Peter and Joyce Butler, and Tracy Chadwick (medical herbalist) of Saxon Village Crafts; Anthony Barton, medieval musical instrument consultant; Bob Powell at the Weald and Downland Open Air Museum, Sussex; Steve Hollick and Chris Kemp, and all members of the National Guild of Stonemasons and Carvers, London; Caroline Benyon at Carl Edwards Studio; the Department of Medieval and Later Antiquities at the British Museum, London; the Museum of London; Jon Marrow at Norton Priory Museum Trust; the Dean and Chapter of York; All Saints Church, North Street, York; St Nicholas Church, Stanford-on-Avon; Castle Museum Norwich, Norfolk Museums Service; Susila Baybars for editorial help; Joe Hoyle and Cormac Jordan for design help; David Graham for endpapers; Charlotte Webb for proofreading; Peter Radcliffe and Steve Setford for the wallchart; Jo Little, Lisa Stock, and Jessamy Wood for the clipart CD.
Additional photography by Peter Anderson (40bc, 49cl, 52c, bl, 55c, 60tr, 61tr); John Chase (42cr, 46–47, 61cl); Andy Crawford (54bl); Steve Gorton (19tr, 32–33c); Peter Hayman, Ivor Kerslake, and Nick Nichols (22cr, 30c, l, 31bl, 42cl, bc); Gary Ombler (38–39)
Model by Peter Griffiths (32–33)
Artworks by Anna Ravenscroft (40); John Woodcock (52–53)

Picture credits:
The Publisher would like to thank the following for their kind permission to reproduce their photographs:

(Key: a-above; b-below/bottom; c-center; f-far; l-left; r-right; t-top)

AKG, London: 6br, 38bc, 61br, 62bl; 64tr; /Photo: Erich Lessing/San Apollinare in Classe, Ravenna, 6lc, /Photo: Erich Lessing/Galleria dell'/Accademia, Florence: 7rc; /Pfarrkirche, Cappenberg: 7bl; /Nuremburg City Library: 19tl; /Bern, Burgerbibliotheque: 21tl; /Bibliothèque de St Genevieve: 31tl; /Bibliothèque Nationale, Paris: 48tr, 56tr, 61tc, 63tr; /Visioars 65cr; **The Art Archive:** /British Library 67bl; /Chiesa di San Francesco Pescia/Dagli Orti 67tl; /Musze Thomas Dobrze Nantes/Dagli Orti 67tr; **Ancient Art & Architecture Collection:** 25bl, 32tr; **Musée des Arts Decoratifs, Paris**/Photo: Sully-Jaulmes: 14c; **Ashmolean Museum, Oxford:** 7c, 45bl; **Avoncroft Museum of Historic Building:** 71tr; **Keith Barley:** 35tl; **Bede's World:** 68c, 68tl, 68bl; **Bridgeman Art Library, London:** /Bibliothèque de la Sorbonne, Paris: 6bl; /Trinity College, Dublin: 6tr; /British Library, London: 7tc, 9br, 10br, 10bl, 12br, 14cl, 15bl, 20tr, 22cl, 23cl, 24br, 30tl, 31tr, 36b &c, 42br, 43cl, 45cl, 50br, 50cl, 51cl, 54br, 58c, 60br/ With special authorisation of the City of Bayeux: 7tl; /Victoria & Albert Museum, London: 8tr;/Musée Condée, Chantilly, /Giraudon: 12tr, 17tr, 30bc, 60bl; /Vatican Library,
Rome: 15tl; /Fitzwilliam Museum, University of Cambridge: 15cl, 27bl; /Bibliothèque Nationale, Paris: 22tr, 27tl, 28tr, 45tc, 54c; /Kunsthistorisches Museum, Vienna: 24bc; /Department of the Environment, London: 25tl; /Westminster Abbey, London: 26tr; /Sixt Parish Church, Haut-Savoie, France: 31br; /Galleria degli Uffizi, Florence: 35br; /San Francesco Upper Church, Assisi: 37tl; / Qu'ran with Naskh script, 1468, Persian School, (15th cent.)/© The Trustees of the Chester Beatty Library, Dublin 41tc; /Seminario Patriarcale, Venice: 47bl; /Staatsarchiv, Hamburg: 47tc; / British Museum: 48bl; /Bibliothèque Royale de Belgique, Brussels: 48c; /City of Bristol Museum & Art Gallery: 62bl; /Bibliothèque de l'Institut de France, Paris/Giraudon: 63tl; **British Library, London:** 53br, 54cr, 54tl, 56c, 62c, 66–67; **British Museum, London:** 27r, 30bl, 45tr, 69cl, 69c, 69br; **Jean-Loup Charmet, Paris:** 41tl, 42tr; **Musée de Cluny, Paris:** 62bc; **Corbis:** Bettmann 67br; **Danish National Museum, Copenhagen:** 6c; **Dorling Kindersley:** Museum of London 22tl; Rough Guides/Demetrio Carrasco 44tr; **The English Heritage Photo Library:** 68br; E.T. Archive, London: 24ac, 29tc, 34tl; /Victoria & Albert Museum, London: 11br, 11cr, 16tl; /British Library, London: 14tr; /Biblioteca Marciana: 22bl; /Bibliothèque Nationale, Paris: 28cl; /Biblioteca Estense, Modena: 38c; /Collegio del Cambio, Perugia: 46cl; /Biblioteca Augustea, Perugia: 53tr; **Mary Evans Picture Library, London:** 24tr, 66crb; /Institution of Civil Engineers: 66tr; **Werner Forman Archive, London:** /Metropolitan Museum of Art, NewYork: 45br; Photographie: Giraudon/Bibliothèque Nationale, Paris: 8tl; Sonia Halliday & Laura Lushington Photographs/ Victoria & Albert Museum, London: 12c ; **Sonia**
Halliday Photographs: 35c, 58tr; **Robert Harding Picture Library:** 7br, 26br, 33tl, 40br, 51tl, 56bl; **Michael Holford:** 14bl; **Museum of London:** 52bc; **Puffin Books:** Churches & Cathedrals by Helen Leacroft, 1957. Reproduced by permission of Penguin Books Ltd.: 33tr, 33cr; **Scala, Florence:** /Archivo di Stato, Siena: 8lc;/ Muséo dell' Opera del Duomo, Orvieto: 50tl, 50bl, 51br, 51tr; **Sir John Soane's Museum, London:** 33br, 70m; **Trinity College Library, Cambridge:** 39tr; **Wallace Collection:** 25tr, 49tl; **Woodmanserne:** 61bl; **Zefa Pictures:** 48br.

Wallchart:
Keith Barley: www.barleystudio.co.uk / St. Nicholas Church, Stanford-on-Avon cl (window); **Dorling Kindersley:** Courtesy of the Anthony Barton Collection cb (lute), clb (purse); Courtesy of the Ashmolean Museum, Oxford fcla; Courtesy of the Weald and Downland Open Air Museum, Chichester ftr; Geoff Dann / Dean and Chapter of York ftl (Bishop), ftl (King), ftl (Lord); Laurence Pordes / Courtesy of The British Library cla (scribe); Peter Anderson / Courtesy of Saxon Village Crafts, Battle, East Sussex bc; Courtesy of Warwick Castle, Warwick crb (helmet)

Jacket: Front: Dean Conger/Corbis, b; **Tony Barton Collection,** tl; **Museum of London, UK,** tcl; **Dean and Chapter of York, UK,** tcr; **Weald and Downland Open Air Museum, UK,** tcr. **Back: All Saints Church,** br, c; **Ashmolean,** br; **British Museum,** cr; **Museum of London,** br.

All other images © Dorling Kindersley.
For further information see:
www.dkimages.com